CAN MOVIES
BE A MORAL COMPASS?

PETER MALONE

Can Movies be a Moral Compass?

ST PAULS

ST PAULS Publishing
187 Battersea Bridge Road, London SW11 3AS, UK
www.stpauls.ie

Co-published with the World Association for Christian Communication

Copyright © ST PAULS and WACC 2005

ISBN 085439 713 2

Set by TuKan DTP, Fareham, Hampshire, UK
Printed in Malta by Progress Press Company Limited

ST PAULS is an activity of the priests and brothers
of the Society of St Paul who proclaim the Gospel
through the media of social communication

Contents

Foreword	7
Introduction – Can movies be a moral compass?	11
Bamboozled	17
The Seamless Robe of Life	45
Who Says We Don't Need Another Hero?	77
Serendipity	105
Priests on a Pedestal – and Priests Toppled	133
Afterword	173
The World Association for Christian Communication	175

Foreword

Film has universal appeal. Everyone succumbs to the magic of the moving image, a form of escapism that is, at the same time, both communication and communion. Films are experienced individually and collectively. They transcend time and space. Like music, they can be understood without specialist knowledge – a true form of democratic communication. And films are fun.

'The film-maker is no longer the competitor of the painter and the playwright, he is, at last, the equal of the novelist', writes André Bazin.[1] In other words, the film-maker is a story-teller, who uses the juxtaposition of images to explore human consciousness and self-understanding.

Story-telling is as old as humankind. The third century BC Mesopotamian story of *Gilgamesh*, the legends of ancient Greece (for centuries recited from memory and finally written down by Homer), the Hindu *Mahabharata*, African griots, Chekhov, Maupassant, Somerset Maugham, John Steinbeck, Eduardo Galeano – all bear witness to the insatiable human thirst for stories. Cinema renders stories (words about deeds) into images, revealing human strengths and weaknesses, probing the mysteries of life and death. The film-maker shows us how we act as human beings and raises questions that we might not wish to confront in reality. In this respect, cinema plays both an ontological role (exploring the nature of being) and a theological role (exploring our relationship – or the lack of it – with God).

Cinema – the moving image – changes society. It has profound effects on the way society sees itself and the way people respond to moral and social issues, e.g. capital punishment (*Dead Man Walking*), abortion (*Vera Drake*), gay rights (*The Wedding Banquet*), old age (*On Golden Pond*), youth (*Cidade de Deus*), disability (*Children of a Lesser God*), the ethical consequences of science (*Terminator, Artificial Intelligence*). It impacts on politics, questioning power relationships (*Fahrenheit 9/11*), highlighting political absurdities (*The Syrian Bride*) and racial prejudices (*Ae Fond Kiss*).

Cinema also changes the way we know about things (our epistemology), e.g. moving images become 'history' and what people remember about the past is what films show them (*Battleship Potemkin, The Passion of the Christ*). Cinema 'rewrites' the past, reinforcing modern myths about nations (*Black Hawk Down*), leaders (*JFK*) and celebrities (*Piaf*), occasionally celebrating genuine heroes (*Romero*) and heroines (*Aung San Suu Kyi*). Cinema explores alternative understandings of the religious (*Star Wars, The Fisher King, The Matrix*) and critiques covert church practices (*The Magdalene Sisters, Priest*).

In a sense the 'language of our time' is the language of the moving image, but the assumption that people can 'read' cinema without any formal training is open to question. Films take positions; they are edited; they offer partial truths. They can be used to reveal and to conceal, for political and socio-cultural propaganda and censorship. That is why people need to learn how to read and reflect critically about what they see, to understand the techniques, syntax and grammar of film, recognising its hidden messages and questioning its assumptions and worldviews. There is a fundamental need for media education about film and for such values-related organisations as INTERFILM and SIGNIS that study and reflect on cinema.

Democracy and culture are also inextricably linked in the domain of cinema, which is why cinema is important for social development. If 'good citizenship' is understood to embody democratic principles and self-understanding at the level of both community and nation, cinema is one way of exploring what it means. Cinema offers images that reinforce Benedict Anderson's notion of 'imagined communities', '*imagined* because the members of even the smallest nation will never know most of their fellow-members, meet them, or even hear of them, yet in the minds of each lives the image of their communion.'[2]

As public communication, cinema dialogues about human dignity and can be used to strengthen the human rights that underlie it. The danger is, as all too many films show, that the medium can also be used to denigrate or abuse those rights. At its best, however, film is the means of social development *par excellence*. It tells stories of human achievement and failure. It explores relationships, identities, and the grand themes of life. Above all, it shows us what it means to be human.

Philip Lee

NOTES

1. Bazin, André (1967). *What Is Cinema?* Volume 1, p.40. Berkeley: University of California Press.
2. Anderson, Benedict (1991). *Imagined Communities: Reflections on the Origin and Spread of Nationalism*, p.5. Revised edition. London and New York: Verso.

Philip Lee studied modern languages at the University of Warwick, Coventry, and conducting and piano at the Royal Academy of Music, London. He joined the staff of the World Association for Christian Communication in 1975, where he is director of the Global Studies Programme and editor of the international journal *Media Development*. Recent publications include *Requiem: Here's Another Fine Mass You've Gotten Me Into* (2001); and *Many Voices, One Vision: The Right to Communicate in Practice* (ed.) (2004).

INTRODUCTION

Can movies be a moral compass?

The title of this introduction would probably elicit the answer 'no' were it put to a range of people in the street. In fact, many of them might suggest that movies were an 'immoral compass'. But this is what some anthropologists and some horror movie buffs would call an 'urban legend'.

In fact, at the end of 2004, the four films that had performed outstandingly at the US box-office and all around the world, the films that millions of people paid tickets for and then paid more millions for video and DVD copies were, in order of bankability, *Shrek 2, The Lord of the Rings: The Return of the King, Spiderman 2* and *The Passion of the Christ*. Number five was *Harry Potter and the Prisoner of Azkhaban*, but its receipts were almost $100,000,000 behind *The Passion*.

These successful films are not immoral compasses. Rather, they are the films that millions everywhere flocked to see and then rushed to own. *Shrek 2* was a delight. *The Lord of the Rings* trilogy reminded the public and the movie moguls that, deep down, audiences responded well to quests, to tales of moral decision-making and the archetypal aspects of myth that stimulate imagination beyond the day-by-day world, yet bring us back to earth with a sharpened moral sense for our own lives. *Spiderman 2* offered a comic book hero who had more depth than might be expected and who was committed to combating evil even if it meant sacrificing his own ambitions and lifestyle to achieve this.

Not everyone was moved by Mel Gibson's depiction of

the passion of Jesus, many finding its torture and bloodshed too much to take. But more than a sufficient number of people found the film a timely reminder of what they appreciated in the Gospels and in Jesus' supreme self-giving for the human race in his crucifixion. In fact, for Lent and Easter 2004, how could clergy compete with *The Passion* standing in their pulpits and trying to preach merely in words?

The comparison between pulpit and screen is a relevant and arresting one. Church leaders frequently remind their congregations, even when they are in favour of 'lights, camera, faith', that the cinema is no substitute for the church, the screen for the pulpit. This is strictly true. However, statistics and emptier churches remind us that millions are buying tickets to enjoy and reflect on films. They signal an unequivocal message that an imagination trained in an audiovisual culture will need a different and new kind of evangelisation, instruction or catechesis today.

I was invited to write this book by Philip Lee, director of the Global Studies Programme of the World Association for Christian Communication (WACC). He believes that we should be exploring films and their values. In recent years, I have been heading SIGNIS, the World Catholic Association for Communication. For a long time I have reviewed films and firmly believe in their power and impact for exploring values. This book is a step in ecumenical collaboration. But, it was not just to be written for our respective churchgoers. Everyone can see a film, go to a cinema, watch it on television, rent or buy a DVD. The conversation initiated in this book is a conversation open to everyone. What are the values we respond to in a film? How is a film an alternative pulpit? How are so many of today's films moral compasses?

A moral compass?

The first thing to say, of course, is that it is the stories. They may be classic in their narrative, they may be avant-garde in their look and their sound, they may be post-modern in their structure (Quentin Tarantino has had more influence than many might like to admit) – but they are stories. Within the space of two hours, more or less, we enter into the world of the film, accept the genre that it belongs to along with the conventions that make it work, identify with characters favourable or unfavourable, and share moral questions and dilemmas. We are also challenged in our senses, our emotions, our wills and our minds, to appreciate the values in the film. Sometimes the values are evident (sometimes even didactic or emotionally manipulative). At other times, we check on our own values because of our disagreement with, even disgust at, those on screen. But, we also need to remember that human nature is redeemable no matter what moral dead-ends and byways people stumble into.

Psalm 130 offers us a lead for understanding these grimmer films, the films that portray characters losing their ways. The psalm begins, 'De profundis', 'out of the depths I cry to you, O Lord, Lord, hear my voice'. These are the 'De profundis' films that challenge all audiences, especially believers, to try to understand the need for compassion and forgiveness. In this way, so many films have compass points that direct us to ways of salvation. It is what Jesus did in telling the story of the father who loved and forgave his son, the prodigal, after he returned out of the depths of his wasted life in the foreign land.

A spiritual compass?

One of the interesting aspects of interviewing movie people, especially film directors, is asking them about religion. Most of them say that they have no religion or have lost touch with the religion of their childhood. They then hasten to add that they have a spirituality. This is what many parents and grandparents say about their children: they don't practise their religion anymore – but they are still spiritual. With the credibility of authority, both secular and religious, in a diminished state, so many people, especially in Western cultures, are either giving up on religion or taking refuge in it so that it will provide unchanging securities.

We cannot underestimate the spiritual longings of the human heart. Thomas Aquinas listed these longings as one of the basic human drives (the others being to live, to love and to live in society). The search for values, for something or someone transcendent is a spiritual drive that is still powerful in our allegedly secularised world. This is what the movies pick up on. This is the dramatising of values, of parable-telling on screen, whether the parables offer spiritual and moral guidance (answer parables) or whether they challenge audiences to re-appraise their stances (question parables). In these ways, movies can serve as a spiritual compass.

Response to films today reminds us how the issue of images and language can be divisive. Consider the differences between the language of the churches and the language of young people today. It is not just the language of young people!

An important part of people's language today, no matter where they live and what their culture, is the audio-visual language that has developed during the last fifty years, especially through the pervasive presence of television. It means that we all take for granted the language of the media that expresses our day-to-day experience. Yet, so much of church and religious language is remote or technical. The challenge for those involved in religious education of all kinds, pulpit, classroom, home, is to foster the meeting between audiovisual language and images and the traditional language of doctrine, morality and church business. What can emerge is language and audiovisual images that express spirituality and can communicate with the broadest audience in a contemporary and relevant way.

Cinema is a significant part of this audiovisual language. It is popular in movie houses, on television, on cassette and DVD and on the Internet. It is available. It is enjoyed. Audiences want to talk about their responses, test their reactions, explore the issues and questions. This book looks at some of these issues.

One of the greatest preoccupations of our time is the relationship between religion and science. As the sciences have developed in recent centuries, we have come to expect continual breakthroughs, knowledge and exploration of the universe, industrial revolutions, technological advances from skyscraper to microchip and improvements in health care and biogenetics. While we are in awe of these wonders, we are innately cautious even as we welcome the latest medical headline. The myth of Dr Frankenstein and his giving life to a monster is never far from the surface of enthusiasm along with a suspicion of those who 'play God'. Films illustrating these bioethical themes are considered in the first chapter. Since life and the quality of life relate directly to these scientific issues, the second chapter puts forward some case studies. These are related to what Cardinal Joseph Bernardin referred to as 'the seamless garment of life', a positive morality of each stage of human existence. These case studies consider abortion (*Vera Drake*), abuse (*Mysterious Skin*) and capital punishment (*Dead Man Walking*).

Since the release of *Star Wars* in 1977, there has been an undiminished spate of movies based on comic book characters and the battle between good and evil, whether this be in the galaxies or on the streets of the contemporary American city, whether the hero and heroine have superhuman powers or not and whether the treatment is realistic or apocalyptic. The yen for the heroic is looked at in the third chapter. While we do not always find saviours coming down our street to save us, we have in recent decades rediscovered guardians from the spiritual spheres. There has been a resurgence of interest, both religious and secular, in angels. Angels appear in the fourth chapter.

In discussions on the planning of this book, one of the issues raised was specifically religious, specifically 'churchy'. It was the treatment of priests and clergy in the movies. There was a time when they were treated with great reverence and respect, images of Fr Spencer Tracy and Fr Bing Crosby. How greatly this has changed. With the critique of authority and authoritarianism in every walk of life, with the demand that authority figures be authentic and give sound reasons for what they ask of others, the priesthood has been opened up for often severe scrutiny. With the publicity given to misconduct stories and the emergence of the extent of clerical sexual abuse, especially of minors, the image of the priest has been tarnished. And this is reflected in the movies, especially since the 1990s. The final chapter of this book presents an overview of the image of the priest in seventy years of cinema.

In looking at some of the crucial questions of our times through the movies, we are doing our bit to foster moral and spiritual growth.

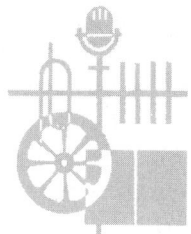

CHAPTER 1
Bamboozled

That is how many people feel when they listen to discussions about genetic engineering, about biotechnology, about advances in medical procedures, and about experiments with human beings. On the one hand, it sounds as if we are destined to live in a brave new world of the elimination of illness and of long, even everlasting, life. On the other, it sounds as if this could turn out to be a bizarre new world of harmful side-effects that return to destroy people years after their medication or surgery, a world of the mutant disabled. Most of us would have to admit that we have little idea of the technical details of what we hear. We depend on the reputations of the experts for their credibility. We find that we depend, often, on our emotional responses to the wonderful promises of a better and healthier life and that we do not ask ourselves about the consequences, especially long-term harmful consequences. We sometimes feel quite bamboozled.

This is the prospect for the twenty-first century. Headline after headline can excite us or alarm us. Is cloning a human being something that would improve life on earth or is it the beginning of a moral and psychological nightmare? For many of us, it is the science fiction movies that offer us some insights into these issues. They are not treatises. They are not sermons (well, some of them may have preaching ambitions). They are stories. They introduce us to the issues, elicit our emotional responses and give us something to think about. And they enable us to discuss these issues more easily and readily with friends or at a more serious level. It is not answers that they provide, rather a stimulus to pursue matters further.

Probably the best place to start is with the character who has given his name to the monstrous dimensions of genetic engineering: Dr Victor Frankenstein. Mary Shelley's novel was published in 1818 and has coloured the popular Western imagination ever since. She described it as 'a new and fearful genre for a new and fearful time'. Victor Frankenstein was the epitome of scientific hubris, an overweening obsession with creating life, not of 'playing' God but of doing what God had done. For those who would like to enter Mary Shelley's world, two films dramatised the summer of 1818 when Byron, Polidori, Shelley and Mary indulged their imaginations and Frankenstein came to life: *The Haunted Summer* (1988) and a typical Ken Russell phantasmagoria, *Gothic* (1986).

The nineteenth century writers who most influenced the futuristic imagination, however, were not the authors who followed her lead. Rather, it was novelists like Jules Verne and H.G. Wells (to name two authors quickly and eagerly taken up by movie-makers) who were popular during the century of progress with its ever-increasing technological inventions in the aftermath of the industrial revolution and the development of machines. At the end of the nineteenth century, Bram Stoker combined the fascination with the monstrous and horror creating Dracula, while situating his contemporary incarnation within the economic growth of Britain and the empire as well as the scientific and technological leaps of the 1880s and 1890s. This is strikingly illustrated in Francis Ford Coppola's classic *Bram Stoker's Dracula* (1992). Robert Louis Stevenson was to do the same, though with a narrower health and psychological focus, in Dr Jekyll and Mr Hyde, another story that has been frequently filmed. On a lighter, almost more frivolous note, Stephen Sommers wrote and directed a horror-adventure-romp, *Van Helsing*, which included Frankenstein and his monster, a cameo by Dr Jekyll while focussing on Dracula.

While the twentieth century was a period of technological development in transport, communications and computers as well as in devastating weaponry, it was a period of development in the discovery of drugs, of medication, surgery and all kinds of medical 'procedures' and experiments for the quality of human life. The twentieth century saw many benign and many sinister Dr Frankensteins. For our purposes, it is interesting to look at the twentieth-century movie history of Frankenstein to realise how this tradition has permeated our imaginations. It plays on our subconscious fear of change that could veer out of control. It activates the innately conservative and cautious elements in the human psyche.

In the 1930s, Universal Studios in Hollywood produced a number of small budget films that have become horror classics. Along with three Frankenstein movies, *Frankenstein* (1931), *Bride of Frankenstein* (1935) and *Son of Frankenstein* (1939), they made *Dracula* (1930) with Bela Lugosi. Dracula, however, is not a creature of life, rather he is the undead, the living dead – with Dracula and vampires we see creatures who play the devil rather than play God.

Audiences were caught up in the activities in Dr Frankenstein's old-fashioned laboratory, the skylights open to the night, waiting for the storms that would produce lightning and the electric power that would bring the doctor's reconstructed creature to life. Unlike God, who is said to have brought Adam to life by the power of his creative spirit, where God breathes life into the man and the woman so that they are made in the image and likeness of God and to live in harmony with nature, Dr Frankenstein is a body snatcher who carries out his experiments in secret, whose creature is a dead criminal who will cause havoc and destruction when he is unleashed.

Mary Shelley saw Dr Frankenstein as arrogant and blasphemous, exploiting science for his own reputation and achievement rather than offering something of value to the human race. While we honour scientists who contribute to human health and well-being, lurking below the surface of our consciousness is this symbol of science gone wrong, experiments gone berserk.

Mary Shelley had sympathy for the monstrous creature. It was not his fault that he had been brought to life. A telling sequence from the original Frankenstein film showed the creature near a river where an innocent little girl is playing. He wants to join her, make flower chains. So delighted is he that in his embracing of the child, he smothers her. This sequence was often cut when the film was first screened, reducing the creature to a heartless monster as audiences saw only the dead body and the townspeople turning into vigilantes bent on destroying him. This meant that Dr Frankenstein's experiment was seen as horrific and dangerous (as it was) but the traces of humanity in the creature were eliminated.

The consequent fear has manifested itself in odd ways in the movies. After the initial scares wore off by the end of the 1930s and world war had broken out, it was time for laughing at one's fears. It was a period of broad comedy and satire. Popular comedians of the time sent up the monsters: *Abbot and Costello meet Frankenstein* (1948, with the credit, 'from the novel Frankenstein by Mary Shelley' – who would have been mightily surprised to see Dracula and the Wolf Man turning up as well). During the 1950s Abbot and Costello also 'met' the Killer, Boris Karloff, Dr Jekyll and Mr Hyde and The Mummy. In those years, audiences were reticent about horror films. The war had provided too many real horrors.

By the late 1950s, it was time to see a more frightening Frankenstein again, this time courtesy of the British Hammer Films who followed the example of Universal in the 1930s. Hammer films were small budget and relied on regular casts of British character actors. Their horror films were in colour, gave more attention to costumes and décor than did Universal and often featured Peter Cushing as Dr Frankenstein and Christopher Lee as the monster. In the Hammer films, the monster was more frightening than sympathetic and audiences during the 1960s and 1970s had a more hostile attitude towards the monster.

There was no let up in audience eagerness for Frankenstein stories during the 1970s and 1980s. With the popularity of television movies, many actors could try their hand as Dr Frankenstein. Gradually, the films went back to a closer reading of Mary Shelley's novel, especially with the final destination of the monster, now more often called 'creature', in the Arctic snows. By 1993, the Frankenstein story could be made into a big-budget, up-market film, produced by Francis Ford Coppola (who had the previous year given greater cinema status to the principal vampire with his *Bram Stoker's Dracula*) and directed by Kenneth Branagh. The author's name became part of the title, *Mary Shelley's Frankenstein*. Branagh played the role of the doctor and Robert de Niro, the creature. Once again, the creature became an object of compassion as well as horror and the critique of the hubris of the doctor was significant. This was a Frankenstein for the end of the twentieth century where audiences could accept Mary Shelley's story as a human drama as well as a spectacle with touches of horror and were profoundly interested in the ethics of genetic engineering and its consequences.

It is helpful to examine different cinema explorations of this basic story to appreciate what are the bioethical and moral concerns of today.

Cloning: *The Sixth Day*

Ira Levin was one of the first authors to bring cloning to the attention of the popular audience. He wrote *The Boys from Brazil*, a fiction where the Nazi doctor of death, Josef Mengele, has fled to Latin America where he has pursued his experiments to clone more Hitlers and unleash the renewed Third Reich. The film version surprised audiences by having the usually upright Gregory Peck as Mengele with Laurence Olivier as his Simon Wiesenthal-type nemesis. His other book was lighter in touch, *The Stepford Wives*, where men used some genetic engineering to transform their wives into robotic clones of themselves, turning them into old-fashioned women's magazine dolls. The film combined satire and horror. Some of the Hollywood moguls thought the issues were still relevant, even if the horror is no longer topical and postmodern satire is the tone, and *The Stepford Wives* was remade in 2004 with Nicole Kidman.

At the end of the Millennium, Arnold Schwarzenegger had appeared in the devil-confrontation thriller, *End of Days*. It quoted the final book of the Bible for its message of good overcoming evil, the Book of Revelation. A year later, in the millennium year, anticipating 'the near future' of the twenty-first century, with a quotation from the first book of the Bible, Genesis, he appeared in a film about creation, humans creating their own images, *The Sixth Day*. The sixth day was when God created male and female in the divine image. In the film, the sixth day refers to future legislation, enacted after some experiments with human cloning, aimed at outlawing such experiments. *The Sixth Day* takes on the very serious issue of cloning, both of animals and humans and the repercussions for individuals and society.

Arnold is (with rapid symbolism) Adam, an ace helicopter pilot, a genial family man with a wonderful wife and daughter. On his birthday, he swaps duty with his buddy to ferry a millionaire involved in genetic engineering. This begins a nightmare in which he becomes the subject of a desperate experiment and has to confront his cloned self. This means, of course, two Schwarzneggers for the price of one – and for Arnold to be heroic twice over, to be an action hero as well as to be self-sacrificing.

The film makes emotional appeals to audience response to cloning because, in this future world, pets can be cloned – and that is what all kiddies want for their doggies. It is easy to see how the emotional appeal for cloning can be made to the unquestioning childlike part of human nature. But in a world of holograms and virtual reality, for some this is not nearly enough. Robert Duvall portrays a scientist, Dr Weir, who deceives himself into thinking he is doing good by cloning humans. His motivation is that other appeal to the heart, the ill and dying wife whose life can be prolonged by these procedures. The scientist has also become the pawn of a ruthless businessman, Drucker (Tony Goldwyn), and has been resurrecting this tycoon several times as well as his thugs who spend most of the film pursuing both Adams (with plenty of chases by car and helicopter). This is the alternative emotional appeal. The businessman is arrogantly unpleasant (even getting his star footballer cloned to continue a winning streak), obviously the villain who resorts to violence to get his way.

So the film continually reminds us that, despite the niceness of having dead pets back or the cloning of depleted fish colonies for feeding people or, especially, cloning terminally ill people so that they are healthy again, cloning can be deadly dangerous in the hands of the power-hungry and the unscrupulous. There are further questions in the screenplay about human dignity, identity, the soul and the reality of ageing and dying.

The title of the film and the reference to the book of Genesis reminds us that humans have been created in the image of God. Does this mean that the image is of God the creator, that men and women are to be the new creators, taking up where God left off? Have humans been created so that they should 'play God' in dealing with these bioethical issues?

Another problem this film raises concerns the worrying question as to whether clones are fully and truly human? Issues of identity become all-important. Is the clone really, truly and fully the same as his/her original? Can the clone live the same life as the original person – especially in their most private life and the intimacy with their spouse? In *The Sixth Day*, while the real Adam comes to appreciate his clone (after all Adam is a hero), he also sees so many evil characters and their clones. The screenplay has a mixture of Arnold as action hero and Arnold as moralist.

Besides the issue of whether cloning is moral or not, the film reminds its audiences that, even if cloning were approved and desirable, who is it that makes the ultimate decisions and what criteria are to be used. What risks to human life are permissible? How long should attempts at cloning go on with the consequent risk of side-effects? Early in the film, the businessman puts forward a surface plausible argument that cloning is good, citing the benefits for business from his own continued existence as well as that of his star player. On the other hand, in a culminating discussion between Adam and Dr Weir, Dr Weir tries to argue rightly that science is not evil in itself but that evil people can become scientists.

Experience also tells us that every development, good or bad, has been exploited. Here it is unscrupulous and greedy individuals and corporations who play at making these life and death decisions, a presumptuous playing at God.

One of the difficulties that people do not want to face is the legal status of the clone. The film makes an emotional appeal in favour of the person over the clone by showing the clone entering into the family's life, enjoying the party for Adam's daughter and sleeping with his wife. So, if the clone is Adam, does this matter? If not, who is the clone? A further complication is raised because, technically, Adam and the other individuals have been pronounced dead and certificated.

Since *The Sixth Day* is a film and not a philosophical or scientific treatise, the moral issues receive another emotional presentation. Adam's clone does not know what has happened to the actual Adam. They meet and make an agreement about their strategy in confronting Drucker, each taking the other's place, the clone entering Drucker's office who thinks it is Adam (as does the audience), the revelation of a sign in the mouth indicating that he is in reality the clone. Drucker tries to clone himself yet again. But the process is incomplete when Drucker is shot. He wants to hasten the procedure resulting in two Druckers. In a spectacular roof confrontation, Drucker's waiting helicopter is blown apart and he hurtles, shattering the glass roof of his building, to his death. Evil is conquered and destroyed once more.

On the other hand, there is a final plea for the good side of cloning. Adam bids farewell to his clone, expressing gratitude for saving him and offering his family as the clone's family.

There is one more irony. The clones had been injected with diseases, submitted to laboratory experimentation with permission – or does a clone need to give permission? To help the audience cope with all this information they have received and the emotional turmoil they have been put through, the film shows a memory disk which recapitulates the whole plot.

Even though films like *The Sixth Day* come and go, they bring serious issues to the general public, always with the Frankenstein warning that monsters, even sympathetic monsters, can be created.

Another clone-warning film is *The Godsend* (2004). When a seven-year-old boy, Adam, is accidentally killed by a truck, a sympathetic doctor approaches the parents at the funeral offering to clone their son. It is to be secret and the family has to move to be near the doctor's Godsend institute. They agree, the mother desperate to have her son again, the father reluctant. All goes well until the boy (Adam again) reaches the age at which he died. He also seems to be possessed at times by another boy, a violent and ruthless boy – which, in a heightened melodramatic confrontation, turns out to be the dysfunctional son of the doctor who wanted his own son to find a new body. This is all the more sinister as Robert de Niro is the doctor and the 'playing God' and hubris theme is strongly developed in the confrontation with the parents at the end. Another cautionary tale that no matter how worthy the motives, there are always evil intentions lurking behind the scenes.

Weapons: *The Lawnmower Man*

The Lawnmower Man is a science fiction thriller that stages its climactic battle between good and evil in virtual reality. The film is based on a Stephen King short story (though King is alleged to have disowned the film). It is another variation on the Frankenstein theme. Dr Angelo (Pierce Brosnan) is a scientist who experiments with the effect of virtual reality on monkeys and developing increased intelligence. He is forbidden by the Government to pursue his investigations.

He lives next door to a church where a simple-minded gardener, named Jobe (Jeff Fahey), mows the lawns and cleans the church. He often talks to Jesus on the large crucifix in the church. He lives in a room on the grounds of the rectory where the parish priest is a sadistic tyrant (and would be in the courts these days), who flogs Jobe to teach him discipline and obedience. Obviously, Jobe's name is more than symbolic. The scientist decides to continue his experiments with Jobe – and finds that he has created a sophisticated man who is far more intelligent than he.

This is not the end of the story. This film comes from the early 1990s, the end of the cold war where conspiracy tales (like those by Robert Ludlum) fed the eager imagination of espionage aficionados. One of the features of conspiracy theories, especially concerning the CIA and the Pentagon, is that they are always on the lookout for a means to create superhuman human weapons (while decrying the military dedication of terrorist suicide bombers). The scientist does not know it, but the experiments are being controlled by the military. Jobe (and his intelligence) are contaminated.

Jobe now has the ability to recognise what is happening to him in the experiments, to explain the development of his mind. He has the capacity to levitate objects. He attempts to invade Dr Angelo's mind. As Jobe excels, Angelo appears more and more human, helpless. The creator loses control of his creation.

Brett Leonard's thriller culminates in a literal countdown before a bomb explodes. During the countdown, Jobe and the scientist enter virtual reality where they confront each other, creating computer graphics and where some of the tactics become impossible, 'Access Denied'. Jobe is now dressed in black, the scientist in white. Jobe declares that he is very angry with his 'maker' and claims that he now is God. His strategy is to put his opponent on a cross. The result is the virtual torture and crucifixion of the scientist – until Jobe himself is destroyed.

In 1992, this was comparatively new and exciting technology, even if the hidden preparation of humans as weapons was familiar enough. The religious dimensions give the film a stronger quality. Jobe, like his Old Testament counterpart, suffers without complaint. He is punished by the sadistic priest (whom the new God-like Jobe destroys by mind-control, standing ominously in the church gallery, telekinetically setting the priest alight beneath the crucifix he once confided in, like an avenging angel turning the priest into a live burning cross). With the connection to the crucifix, the innocent and simple Jobe is seen as a Christ-figure. Ultimately, he endures his own passion not knowing how he has been manipulated.

This is the realm of genetic engineering. While the eugenic experiments of Nazi doctors like Mengele were exposed after World War II, further experiments with drugs continued into the 1960s (and with agent Orange claims after the Vietnam War even later). Our twenty-first century suing-for-compensation culture has alerted the public to the prevalence of this kind of abuse.

During World War II, prisoners were given 'truth drugs' during interrogations. The war in Korea revealed techniques of brainwashing, altering mind states. The classic film dramatising the effect of brainwashing and manipulation was the 1962 version of Richard Condon's frighteningly satiric novel, 'The Manchurian Candidate', where political and financial lobbies used a disturbed war veteran to assassinate a politician. The film featured Laurence Harvey as the assassin and Angela Lansbury as his ruthless mother. The film was released in 1963, the year of John F. Kennedy's assassination in Dallas, and was withdrawn by its star and co-producer, Frank Sinatra, a close friend of the late president. The film was re-released only in the late 1980s.

However, the issue is still of major concern. An updated remake of *The Manchurian Candidate*, with a Gulf War setting, was released in 2004 with Denzel Washington, Meril Streep as the mother and Liev Schreiber as the sleeper agent. This time it was not actual Manchurians who were brainwashing the American soldiers. Rather, it was a US global corporation, Manchurian, which was experimenting with drugs for mind-control, altering the memories of a squad of soldiers during Operation Desert Storm. It is not the Pentagon which is trying to create new human weapons. It is the politicians and the multinationals who want to have their own politicians in power and use their weapons for assassinations to ensure the success of their candidates.

Mutants: *The Island of Dr Moreau*

Novelist H.G. Wells is probably best known for his interest in technological developments. His story of *The Time Machine* was in the Jules Verne exploration genre. He also wrote the futuristic novel, *Things to Come*. He was also interested in the science fiction of genetic engineering. Two of his novels are classics and have been the basis for a number of films, starting as early as the 1930s. They are *The Island of Dr Moreau* and *The Invisible Man*. With their focus on a scientist who wants to go beyond the limits of contemporary science and sets himself up as a new Dr Frankenstein, these stories are part of the cautionary tradition about scientists and hubris and the disastrous results of their experimentation. Dr Moreau experiments on people, turning them into mutants. The Invisible Man experiments on himself. With versions of both stories on screen in the 1930s, the 1970s and the 1990s, it is clear that these stories resonate with modern audiences.

In the 1933 version, called *The Island of Lost Souls*, victims of a shipwreck land on an isolated Pacific island where Dr Moreau has built his secret laboratories. Secret laboratories in the Pacific are not so far-fetched when one remembers that within twenty years, immediately after World War II, the Americans would use the Bikini atoll in the Marshall Islands as the testing ground for nuclear warheads and that the French in the ensuing decades would detonate in the Tahitian islands at Mururoa atoll. The Pacific is a region that suffered the devastation of illnesses introduced from Europe, like smallpox, where the 'civilised' world offloaded its evils on 'the noble savages' of the so-called South Sea paradises.

Dr Moreau has been experimenting with humans and animals. The result: what were called humanimals, mutant creatures where humanity was not destroyed but was trapped in the forms, shapes and bodies of beasts. This is, of course, nightmare stuff. While it was somewhat prophetic in the 1930s, *The Island of Lost Souls* was seen more as a horror film.

When it was remade in 1977 with Burt Lancaster as Dr Moreau, the world had experienced the results of widespread atomic radiation (which led to a whole genre of science-fiction films) as well as physical deformities due to unforeseen side-effects of drugs like thalidomide in the 1960s. It was obviously time for the message of Wells' fable to be listened to again and more attentively. The screen techniques were available to create grotesque creatures that would alarm the audiences as to what could happen. Better known actors, like Michael York, were cast. The film was not an outstanding success and was produced by the rather sensationalist production company, American International Pictures (AIP), but it found its place among the alarmist tales about mad scientists and the havoc they could wreak on the bodies and minds of human beings. The setting is still the Pacific.

It is a pity that the intentions for the 1996 version of *The Island of Dr Moreau* did not translate into the final product. This was big budget film-making, but the result was ludicrous and a financial and critical fiasco. Nevertheless, it reminds us that Wells' story and message were still relevant. This time Dr Moreau was experimenting not just with chemicals, but with DNA itself, and still imprisoning humans as humanimals. If one can sit through the film, the themes are still there to be examined, with Val Kilmer and David Thewliss doing their best but with, of all people, the ultra-large Marlon Brando as Dr Moreau, using the effete voice he sometimes affected and being carried round on the equivalent of a papal *sedia gestatoria*. It is preposterous hamming. With the litigious mentality still current and numerous court cases seeking settlements for the horrible side-effects of drugs that were marketed dishonestly, *The Island of Dr Moreau* could usefully be remade today.

On the other hand, there is a brief sequence in Lindsay Anderson's *O Lucky Man* (1971) that encapsulates the horror in one scene: the audience shares the shock of a hospitalised man who wakes up to find that his head has been surgically attached without his knowledge or consent to the body of a pig.

The Invisible Man

The story of the invisible man is less threatening than that of Dr Moreau. It is a man experimenting on himself rather than on others. What Wells was concerned about, as are the subsequent films, is less the effect of genetic engineering on the body of the scientist than on his mind with the consequent dangers for others. In fact, the invisibility of the body is usually played more for special effects and for touches of comedy. An invisible person can be quite mischievous, playing practical jokes and teasing or tormenting people – but is as elusive as the Scarlet Pimpernel, with everyone trying to seek him here, seek him there, seek him everywhere, to no avail.

In 1933, Claude Rains' invisible man quickly became demented. Initially sincere, he soon discovered his inner shadow and began to use his invisibility for power, even power over life and death and indulging in thrill-killing. This makes this 1933 film (directed by James Whale of Frankenstein fame) quite bizarre.

Sixty years later, the story of the Invisible Man is used to illustrate how accidents can happen with dire results. This time the man rendered invisible is not the scientist trying to aggrandise himself. It is an innocent victim who must try to find a cure. But this is the period of the human weapons films and so the invisible man is pursued by the CIA so that they can use and exploit him. This is John Carpenter's *Memoirs of an Invisible Man* (1992) with comedian Chevy Chase being both serious and funny. He is a desperate side-effect of genetic experimentation.

However, the original hubris warning was repeated with more spectacular special effects, especially for the invisibility, in Paul Verhoeven's *Hollow Man* (2000) with Kevin Bacon as the presumptuous scientist. This time he works with an ambitious team. They are also linked with the Pentagon. Financial grants and the cutting off of funding are big issues now. In the past, the Dr Frankensteins seem to have had at their disposal unlimited resources (even if they had to go out body-snatching for their experiments). In the modern world, the financial motivation is dominant. Grants are limited or refused. Funding is cut. Short-cuts are taken. Experiments are rushed and not properly supervised nor results properly recorded or tested. The possibilities of 'mutant' effects occurring in hospitalisation, in surgery, in mistakes in medication and on the wards seem endless.

Kevin Bacon's *Hollow Man* is brash, brilliant and arrogant. He has little hesitation in submitting himself to his own experiments. While the transition to invisibility is painful and body-racking, he begins to enjoy his ability to see but not be seen (except by special heat/light glasses). But, the cost-cutting and limited time to complete tests mean that it is too difficult to get him back to normal. And, as with Claude Rains archetypal Invisible Man, the mind and soul are contaminated and the invisible man becomes more and more insane, a stalking murderer. As with so many American stories, the film ends with the apocalyptic image, destruction by fire.

These films seem to be warning their audiences against an uncritical optimism. This is not the innocent and good Garden of Eden and the scientists, like Adam and Eve, cannot resist the temptation to eat of the fruit of the tree of knowledge of good and evil. And, again like Adam and Eve, they are thrust out to fend for themselves, trying to find grace in this outer world and handing on to their successors an original sin of hubris. *Hollow Man* might echo the concerns of Wells a hundred years ago, but with the ultra-modern trappings of state of the art education and equipment, it is the same message delivered for a more scientifically sophisticated world.

While the Invisible Man story shows us the scientist breaking free of the limits of being seen but yet finding the monster within, Robert Louis Stevenson's cautionary fable, *Dr Jekyll and Mr Hyde* (which has been filmed in more versions and cinema mutations than either of Wells' stories) has the scientist remaining visible – but unrecognisable. The Invisible Man becomes victim of the evil within and lurks unseen, Dr Jekyll also becomes the victim of the evil within and becomes invisible while Mr Hyde becomes visible. Mr Hyde is an 'altered state' of Dr Jekyll. Earlier films made Hyde look, sound and behave like a monster. Other versions have Hyde as more presentable than Jekyll, all the more deceiving because of his visible charm, which, of course, is a mask of evil.

While these stories work on the level of science, they can also serve in our heavily addicted society to warn of the genetic damage of drugs, whether so-called recreational or designer drugs as well as dependence on medical prescriptions. But that would be another chapter. Eugene O'Neill, in chronicling the dependence of his mother, called this harrowing experience *Long Day's Journey into Night*.

The Heroes

The theme of mutation is explored in ambiguous ways in the stories of the contemporary heroes and heroines from comic books. The X men and women have superhuman strength because of accidents due to experiments. Hugh Jackman is a dashing hero, even in his appearance as Wolverine, the chief of the X Men, but he is still a mutant, a creature who has absorbed some of this animal nature and who struggles with his memories, trying to recapture those that have been lost or stolen from him. The others have had their vision altered and have laser sight, or the ability to fly or to exercise telekinetic powers. They belong to an academy of mutants who are employed to combat a group of malevolent mutants. This kind of heroism in creatures who are humans with a twist, an aberration in their genetic code, was so popular with audiences that X 2 was even more successful than the original.

This is akin to the accident that Peter Parker in *Spider-Man* has when he is bitten by a mutant spider during his class outing to the laboratory. As the venom is absorbed into his blood, he finds that he can scale walls, his fingers can create web and fling it to form a safe and flexible cord. He possesses superhuman strength. Once again, the sequel was even more successful than the original.

The pathos of this kind of mutant film is not so much the effect of the mutation because that is used for heroism and for the good and safety of others but the diminishment of the human, the exhaustion, the toll of the heroics. It is also the diminishment of the psyche as the hero struggles with new questions of identity as well as the secrecy and the isolation that this 'vocation' to help others requires. This is the sacrifice that Peter Parker is prepared to make. We are greatly relieved, however, when we see him reveal the truth to Mary Anne. No matter the wonderful deeds of daring, deep down audiences want him to be able to live an ordinary, 'normal' human life. Once again, audience response to the wonders of science is still cautionary.

Robots, Androids and Cyborgs: HAL, Robbie and the others

A final focus for this chapter, emphasising how much audiences value life and put their trust in the promises of science despite their caution, is the effort that scientists put into machines in order to make them 'more human'.

One of the side-effects, so to speak, of the *Star Wars* phenomenon was the affection generated for the two androids, C3PO and R2D2. While they were the equivalent of mechanical toys, they were treated as brothers. *Star Wars* anthropomorphised their voices, their feelings, their worries (and C3PO's fussiness), their contribution to the battles. It was very important for them to survive and, if 'wounded', to be repaired as quickly as possible.

Star Trek fans were used to this kind of thing with Spock. The first *Star Trek* movie was released in 1979, two years after *Star Wars*. While Spock was a hero and indispensable for the work of the Enterprise, he was still less than human. He could not feel. He did not understand emotions.

There has been a tradition of robots and androids that has embraced the human-friendly machines as well as the human-menacing creations. Robbie the Robot was a delightful creation who gave screen robots their initial credibility in *The Forbidden Planet* (1956). On the other hand, the baleful red light that was the Cyclops-like eye of Kubrick's *2001: A Space Odyssey* (1968) HAL (along with his suavely sinister voice) ensured that he was one of the most threatening of machines. (Commentators always remind us that if we move forward one letter for HAL, we get IBM.)

Perhaps the major screen development of the humanising of the machines was James Cameron's creation, *The Terminator*. In 1984, he was the perfect humanoid or cyborg sent from the future to destroy the child who would grow up to be the warrior-saviour of the humans who would destroy the machines. The Terminator was evil, murderous. As embodied by Arnold Schwarzennegger, he was a human body-built actor playing a superhuman body-built machine. The Terminator had to be destroyed to save the human race.

Trends change and by the time the Terminator fulfilled his promise, 'I'll be back', there was a move towards toning down the amount of screen violence. *Terminator 2: Judgment Day* was one of the most successful films of 1991. This time Schwarzenegger, moving towards his political status as good-guy Californian governor, plays a good cyborg. He has come from the future, not to destroy John Connor, the saviour of the future, but to rescue him from the evil terminator, played with cold, unremitting menace by a continually shape-changing Robert Patrick. In this film, John has to teach the good terminator restraint in his use of weapons, that it was not a heroic thing to shoot and kill indiscriminately. Modifying violence was a key to greater humanising of the machines.

Just before his election as governor, Schwarzenegger appeared in the third instalment, *Terminator 3*, which had the added ominous title, The Rise of the Machines (2003). It is the human race against the machines, a theme taken up in the 2004 adaptation of Isaac Asimov's *I Robot*.

Actually, there is a strong precedent for this kind of confusion between human and machine. At the time of its first release, *Blade Runner* (1982) was hailed as a classic of this genre. It was based on a story by now-celebrated writer, Philip K. Dick. Harrison Ford is Deckard, the 2019 LA cop whose task it is, as a blade runner, to hunt down the humanoids created to serve in the space colonies and who have outlived their use-by date. They are referred to as 'replicants'. Website comments struggle with the words to best describe these replicants. They are referred to as humanoids, as human clones, as artificially created humans. Who are they? Have they really any human identity? Are they simply perfectly created human images, replications of humans? The replicants that Deckard hunts are violent, consumed by a will to live and not be destroyed. Their violence is self-defence.

The release version of *Blade Runner* had a voiceover, in the private-eye fashion, by Deckard. When Ridley Scott's director's cut was released over a decade later, the voiceover had been removed. Scott stated that the voiceover had been a studio imposition and he was eager to remove it. One of the main results of this director's cut is that audiences are now unsure whether Deckard himself is human or is, in fact, a replicant, created to track down and eliminate the rogue replicants. Deckard has communicated throughout the film as a human being. Audiences have responded to him in this way. So, what if he is not human? What is human?

Fans of Philip K. Dick will be interested to follow through these themes in several other films made from his writings. The principal films are *Total Recall* (1990), *Imposter* (2002), *Minority Report* (2002), *Paycheck* (2004), *A Scanner Darkly* (2005) and *Next* (scheduled for a 2006 release).

Rekall Inc is the agency in *Total Recall*. It is an institute for the implanting of false memories. When a construction worker (Arnold Schwarzenegger again) experiences an implant of a trip to Mars, things go wrong and an evil personality emerges from his psyche. Once again, the question is who is the real person, the worker or the emerging personality.

Paycheck is concerned with altered mind states and implanted memories, a serum being used that enables business companies to employ computer whizzes to develop programs and delete their memories.

Imposter is akin to *Blade Runner*. This time an engineer constructs androids that can be used as weapons to destroy alien invaders. While this seems to be quite clear, the engineer himself is then suspected of being an android himself and he is pursued by government agents wanting to destroy him. Is he the android? Are the officials and agents androids? Once again, it is the question of who is human and what does it mean to be human.

Minority Report takes us on a slightly different path. Police agencies of the future can prevent crime by using information given them from a select group of extraordinary humans called 'precogs'. They float in a large bath with electrodes on their heads transmitting visions of crimes to come that are transformed into visuals and give the exact information about time, place and perpetrator. Are these dreams infallible? The ace detective (Tom Cruise) discovers that he will commit a murder. Can he stop himself, change time, change the future?

In *A Scanner Darkly*, a policeman (Keanu Reeves) has to deal with a drug that creates multiple personalities.

There is a consistency of theme in these versions of Philip K. Dick stories. Top directors have filmed them, including Steven Spielberg, Paul Verhoeven, John Woo, Richard Linklater. What is human and what is not? How far can humans go in creating humanoids? What is positive, at the service of humans? What is negative, destructive of humanity?

The other question is: how far can humans go in mechanising themselves? We remember the television series of the 1970s where these questions were tantalising and audiences in millions watched *The Six Million Dollar Man* and *The Bionic Woman*. Or, we might experience a flashback to *Dr Strangelove* and wonder whether, as his arm jerks to the Nazi salute, the machine had taken over the man. Perhaps the best film example for pondering this question is the series of *Robocop* films. Once again, we find that Paul Verhoeven (remembering that he directed the later *Total Recall* and *Hollow Man*) made the first film. 'Part man. Part machine. All cop. The future of law enforcement' This was the poster slogan for this story of a Detroit police officer who was severely wounded and returns to the force – relentlessly – as a reconstructed human-cyborg. He can go where others fear to go – into a hail of bullets that dent, bounce and ricochet rather than destroy. This is superman with natural hardware rather than Krypton. If the ideal robot is desirable, then so is the ideal Robocop.

With the development of computer graphics during the 1990s, we have films where the humans are needed only as computer screen prototypes and a thousand extras in *Braveheart* (1995) can become a large army, the audience for the fights in the arena in *Gladiator* (2000) can be technically multiplied, Tom Hanks can become several characters in *Polar Express*, the animation developing the human input. Actually, this reached an extreme in Andrew Nicol's *Simone* (2002). (Nicol wrote *The Truman Show* and *Gattaca*, two other films that speculated on the interface between people and science and technology.) Simone receives two Oscars during the film. She does rock concerts as well. The reality is that she does not exist as a person at all. She is Simulation One, Simone, a computer program who is born on the screen, speaks electronically with infinite human nuances, including the voicing of her creator's thoughts – and can be turned off at will, not a technical murder, merely technological deletion.

A final film for consideration here is *AI: Artificial Intelligence* (2002). The original story is by Brian Aldiss. Stanley Kubrick planned to direct the film but died before this could happen. Kubrick had already indicated his strong interest in this theme with his creation of 2001's computer, HAL. Kubrick had entrusted the project to Stephen Spielberg who adapted Kubrick's screenplay.

Spielberg had been in regular communication with Kubrick over the years and, with this film, wanted to honour his memory. While there are echoes of Kubrick's themes, like the issue of true human freedom from *A Clockwork Orange* and the voyage into the future from 2001, the treatment is very much in the Spielberg vein. Children have always played important and significant roles in Spielberg films, *Close Encounters* and ET especially. In bringing this vision together in AI, Spielberg traces the journey of a lifelike robot child from machine to humanity. AI is the story of David, a 'mecha' (mechanical creation), who has been programmed to 'feel' many human emotional characteristics, who is placed with a foster family, and learns to love. Haley Joel Osment gives an excellent and credible performance as David.

The resulting film is a sometimes uneasy mix of Kubrick classicism and Spielberg storytelling. Audiences who prefer their science-fiction to have the emphasis on the science will like the prologue with its demonstrations of sophisticated robots in a future world threatened by global warming where families are restricted in numbers of children, where plans are made to build David. The ideas of the film are interesting.

But, Spielberg's way of telling his story is to develop the emotional aspects which 'thinkers' will be tempted to dismiss as sentimentality rather than sentiment. This sentimentality is seen to undermine, even eliminate, the tougher, more philosophical questions about what it is to be human and whether this is possible for machines. Those who prefer storytelling to lectures will respond much more positively to AI, identifying with the plight of David as he awakens to the reality of having a mother, Monica (played by Frances O'Connor).

That is only the first part of the film. The second part has David out on his own, encountering a community of robots past their use-by-date who are being hunted down and destroyed for human bloodlust in a futuristic Coliseum. His companion here is a robot designed as a sex-machine, Gigolo (played by Jude Law). This journey becomes a quest for David to discover who has the power to make him human. When he goes to his creator, Professor Hobby's office, he sees a rack of robots, new up-dated Davids. He escapes to Coney Island, to the grotto of the Blue Fairy who reminds him of his 'mother'.

The third part of AI is set in a very distant future. David has waited 2000 years. The robots have survived. The humans have not. Highly sophisticated aliens (who would look at home in *Close Encounters* and *ET*) are the only survivors who, through stored memories and DNA remnants, can reconstruct aspects of the past (echoes of *Jurassic Park*). David still has a lock of Monica's hair, so the aliens reconstruct, for a day, David's memories. He can spend a day with his mother but she can live only 24 hours. She treats him as her real child. As she dies, he has emotions, he weeps – and loves her. Has David become truly human?

A slighter film in this vein is *Bicentennial Man*, based on a story by Isaac Asimov. *Bicentennial Man* was released on the eve of the millennium. It is a futuristic film, but looking forward with some kind of optimism. Given Robin Williams' exuberant style, it is a restrained performance and shows a robot in human form yearning to be fully human, free and recognised as human. The film also makes the point that while robots can live forever, it is important for human beings to live out their term and eventually die as the body decays and their contemporaries also die. The variation on the theme of humanoids and humans is that the robot gets permission of the ruling council to go through a laboratory process to become human. He is able to feel and, like the humans, grow old and die.

Cautionary tales

From the outset, this chapter has made the point that, on the whole, despite attitudes of optimism about advances in science, in medicine and in genetic engineering, the stories we tell ourselves tend to be alarmist. So much can go wrong – and should we trust the experts? Human nature is prone to error and, often, malice – should we trust one another? Selfish motivations can ruin initially selfless projects. Profit and power have destroyed so much that is good. Recent history has shown us that rushed experimentation, poor testing and human error can lead to unwanted and horrific side-effects – should we believe what individuals, companies and the media tell us?

When Carl Jung wrote about psychological type in the 1920s and what he saw were the four principal ways in which people functioned, he offered a useful schema for exploring why we respond to scientific advances in such different ways. Jung suggested that most people were very grounded in the way that they perceived reality. They take in data through the five senses. This data stays with them and they are blessed with attention to the here and now as well as with strong and generally detailed memories. There are others, however, who take in this sense data but do not retain much of it. They give their attention only to what interests them and tend to 'edit out' the rest. They prefer to speculate on possibilities, hunches and connections rather than simply the evidence of the senses. The here and now perceivers are referred to as Sensing people. The possibilities people are referred to as Intuiting people. This is not meant to be a rigid, schematic categorising of people because all of us are continually sensing and intuiting.

However, we tend to have a preference for one or the other. For many, the preference can be quite marked.

As regards decision-making, Jung suggested that we rely on two different styles of criteria and use both. However, we have a tendency to prefer one to the other. Those who like making judgements based on objective criteria he refers to as Thinking people. Principles, logic, cause and effect are significant factors in decision-making. It is a rational function. So also is the other mode of decision-making even though it is referred to as Feeling. The criteria here tend to be in the realm of values, a more personalised, subjective way of coming to judgements where circumstances modify the objectivity and the complexity of persons is taken more into account.

Statistical research indicates that far more people identify with the Sensing preference rather than the Intuiting. Men tend to prefer the Thinking function over women and women the Feeling function. However, this latter statistic is modifying across cultures in recent decades. How does this relate to scientific advances, especially concerning genetic engineering?

Those who function best with Intuitions will be initially more enthused about the possibilities and breakthroughs. Intuitives enjoy imagining and going beyond perceived limits. What if…? You don't need to be Einstein to appreciate that Einstein himself was powerfully intuitive. Intuitives can lead in stretching the mind – and are encouraged by intuitive responses.

But the majority of people do not function immediately in this way. Sensing people want here and now evidence. Detail is important. Testing and verification in the strictest sense will vouch for reliability. While the intuition about possibilities can be exciting, if it is not based on clear, recorded test results then there is cause for suspicion. The danger with the intuitive approach is that detail is not seen as so crucial. It is important but sometimes involves procedures that bog scientists down and delay progress.

So many of the scientific advances are proposed by intuitives. We are always in need of those who can open up horizons and envision ways beyond those horizons. They can persuade others to share in these visions. However, the majority of people want clear proof and ironclad guarantees that the goals are secure, tested over a safe period and are beneficial. It is not just a matter of doing something simply because we can – that is often an intuitive argument where the hunch and its implementation are more exciting than working through the safeguards to prevent experimentation going wrong.

Dr Victor Frankenstein is an intuitive scientist, wanting to share God's intuitions about life and creation. So obsessed is he that he disregards the sound warnings of the more sensing scientists around him.

Matters become more complex when we consider how different people respond at the decision-making level.

Those who prefer Feeling criteria are more likely to assess a technological advance on what it means to them personally and what it might mean in benefits or dangers for those for whom they care. Immediate response to genetic engineering of the foetus to respond to the need for, say, bone marrow tissue for an ill child is to speak out in favour of it to help the stricken child. Broader ethical issues are seen as far less important because of the urgency of the situation and love for the child. Relief of pain is also an immediate concern so that medication that promises this relief is welcomed without too much regard for side-effects.

On the other hand, if a Feeling person detects some danger in a procedure, they can be just as fierce in protest as others are in favour.

The Thinking person takes a cooler and more objective look at what is being done or could be done. Broader issues are important, issues of scientific development, funding, ethical and moral questions. On the one hand, this kind of detachment could mean a thorough study of a scientific development and its implications. On the other hand, it could mean that more personalised arguments were dismissed and a relentlessly single-minded course pursued.

Dr Victor Frankenstein is a Thinking scientist, believing that his commitment to his work is objective and detached. So obsessed is he that his belief that he is working only for the advance of science rejects all warnings of Feeling family and friends around him.

This means that we need to appreciate where we stand ourselves and how our functioning colours the way we respond to scientific advances. Those who are grounded in Sensing and look objectively at matters will normally argue their case with clear evidence and principled logic and appeal to those who share this approach. Those who are grounded in Sensing but look more subjectively at matters will put forward the evidence in connection with benefits or dangers, appealing to those who are persuaded by heart before head.

On the other hand, those who delight in intuitions and look more subjectively at matters will be looking for ideal processes and developments that might benefit the human race (but run the difficulty of being caught up in the ideal without realising practical dangerous consequences). Those who delight in intuitions and look more objectively at matters, will develop the theories and the procedures that will contribute to advances but run the danger of being enthralled by the brilliance of the possibilities at the expense of testing, evidence and experience. It is in the latter that we find the stereotype of the scientist (as well as the mad scientist). This is where we find Dr Frankenstein.

Aldous Huxley chose a quotation from Shakespeare's *The Tempest* to describe an optimistic future, *Brave New World* – but, like all fiction writers, he acknowledged the irony in his title. Unfortunately, in all of us there is, this time in Joseph Conrad's phrase, a heart of darkness.

CHAPTER 2
The Seamless Robe of Life

There used to be an Australian slogan to boost exercise and a healthy lifestyle: Life, be in it. It almost sounds like a truism. However, we do not have to grow too old to realise that living life is a rather complicated process. While most of us love life we know that life is threatened, life is harmed, life is destroyed. In the early years of the twenty-first century, with acts of terrorism sometimes a daily occurrence, we are called on to affirm life and its possibilities.

Political campaigns immediately remind us that not everybody shares the same views on life. Bitter arguments are fought on the right to life, especially of the unborn child. Bitter arguments are fought on the right to terminate the lives of criminals. Civilian casualties of war are accepted as a regrettable but necessary consequence of bombardment. Medical science has devised ways of keeping a comatose person on life support. Should the apparatus be switched off? We speak of the quality of life, but so many countries experience increasing addiction problems.

Faced with what has been called a culture of death, how are we to promote a 'culture of life'?

The late Cardinal Joseph Bernardin of Chicago, who experienced false accusations of sexual abuse of a seminarian, but who later visited and prayed with his accuser when he was dying of AIDS, shared his own terminal cancer with the people of his diocese, wanting to encourage them when they were ill and dying. It was Cardinal Bernardin who used the phrase 'the seamless garment of life' to try to grasp the challenges raised by life issues that can tear society apart. He evoked memories of Jesus and the Gospels, how Jesus wore a seamless robe to his passion. When the soldiers at the foot of the cross divided his garments and threw lots for them, they were unwilling to tear his seamless robe. It was too beautiful and precious.

A spirituality of the seamless garment of life affirms life at every juncture: conception and birth, growth and maturity, illness and health, threats and abuse, dying and death.

Natural Law, Law of Christ

The issues of life are ethical issues. Philosophical principles of right and wrong must be applied to questions. This is especially true of controversial problems. The issues of life are also moral issues. For centuries, theologians have relied on 'Natural Law' theory to resolve problems. Natural Law theory articulates what is seen as an understanding of the harmonious integrity of human intelligence and human functioning of body and spirit. With Natural Law, ethics and moral theology met and formulated norms for moral behaviour. During the twentieth century, Natural Law theory was put under close scrutiny. Scientists, philosophers and theologians came to appreciate that nature was often more complex than Natural Law theologians allowed for, that scholars in the past did not have the means, for instance, to understand how the human body worked.

An abstract principle obviously possesses great clarity. The German philosopher, Emmanuel Kant, wrote about principles of justice and elaborated a philosophy of human nature's 'categorical imperatives'. These are inbuilt, *a priori* moral demands that intelligent people are aware of. They contribute to a categorising and classifying of behaviour and moral offences. This is a duty-focused morality, a morality of obligations to be fulfilled. But questions still remain as to how to apply Natural Law to the tangled situations we find ourselves in. The normative obligations of Natural Law are still the subject of research and debate.

During the latter part of the twentieth century in both Protestant and Catholic traditions, there was a renewed focus on the Gospels as the primary source of moral teaching. Some commentators regretted that Jesus was not clearer and more systematic in his teaching. There were some subjects that he did not touch on himself – as writers on questions of sexual orientation are quick to point out. German theologian, Dietrich Bonhoeffer, urged his students and readers to take the Sermon on the Mount as the blueprint for Christian discipleship. This renowned sermon, which begins with the Beatitudes was not merely an ideal that Jesus offered even though he knew that it was too difficult to live up. Rather, it is an ideal that should be practised – daily. Even if it leads to suffering and death, which it did for Jesus and for Bonhoeffer himself, God is always present, helping with 'costly grace'.

Another German theologian, the Redemptorist Bernard Haering, contributed to a huge change in perspective in the Catholic Church from the 1960s by writing a text on Moral Theology which focused on the Gospel teachings of Jesus. He called it *The Law of Christ*. The law of love that Jesus urged at the Last Supper is the basis of Christian morality: a new commandment I give you – to love one another as I have loved you. This love is the greatest that any person can have for another: a laying down of life kind of love, whether it be in the ordinariness of daily living or in an ultimate sacrifice of one's life. This law of love creates a moral sense that is respectful of others, loving and responsible.

Moral case studies

One of the old ways of assisting students of theology understand and apply moral principles was by means of what was called 'the case study'. A scenario was devised which sought to illustrate the complexities of moral decisions. In some Catholic seminaries the protagonists of these case studies were called Titius and Bertha, the text of the case being in Latin – which had the difficulty of making the case seem remote and artificial, an intellectual exercise to clarify right and wrong rather than an experience of pastoral concern. When these exercises became common in seminaries in the seventeenth century, critics mocked them as 'mere casuistry' or, when devised by Jesuits who conducted many schools and seminaries, the complications were sometimes derided as 'Jesuitical'. This has become the word to define a devious kind of political nit-picking. It does not, of course, do justice to the contribution of the case study.

However, the case study has come into its own, especially in the last fifty years. This has been aided by the popularity of the movies. So many of the films we value are actually moral case studies, set out for us with characters we can identify with, situations that are credible and moral dilemmas which are not always easily and simply solved but which require empathy and delicacy of conscience. Audiences who respond with intelligence and feeling to these movies are engaged in imaginative moral theology.

Unfortunately, many academic moralists dismiss the movies as 'just entertainment' and undervalue the exposition of moral crises they present in the context of the drama. Within the timeframe of two hours plus or minus, utilising the conventions of familiar genres like the domestic drama, the police thriller, the western, science fiction, they draw their audiences into dealing with important moral questions. They take the audience deeper into moral dilemmas than the mere announcing of a succinct moral (but abstract) principle.

In the first letter to the Catholic Church written by a pope on the theme of movies, Pius XI included a sentence that seems to have escaped the notice of so many theology professors: 'Since then the cinema is in reality a sort of object lesson which, for good or for evil, teaches the majority of men more effectively than abstract reasoning…' (Vigilanti Cura, 1936, n. 23).

Actually, when we go back to the Jewish Scriptures and

look at the text of the Decalogue (Exodus 20), we find a set of generally abstract laws. They are sometimes described as 'apodeictic' laws, a word that means that they point out the obligations of the law they announce. In the three chapters that follow (Exodus 21-23), the applications of some of the commands of the Decalogue are spelt out. This is referred to as 'casuistic' law, case law. Even Moses, so to speak, knew that the abstraction of the Decalogue, important as it was as the legal Covenant foundation for the people of Israel, was not sufficient and that human beings needed more concrete understanding of God's law. As a moral theologian used to say in the 1970s when parents became upset because their children were not taught the Ten Commandments: 'Let's take forty minutes to memorise the Commandments, then what...?' You can enunciate a principle, but having it as a guide for life and putting it into practice demands a lot more sincerity and depth.

This chapter will take three films on controversial life issues and examine them as moral case studies. We begin with questions of the beginning of life and consider Mike Leigh's Golden Lion winner at Venice, 2004, *Vera Drake*. We will move on to one of the ugliest threats to the quality of life that has been exposed since the 1990s, the sexual abuse of children. The film is Gregg Araki's *Mysterious Skin* (2004). Finally, we will look at the issue of capital punishment, the state's right or not to take the life of a criminal. An obvious choice is Tim Robbin's film on the work of American sister, Helen Prejean, *Dead Man Walking*, for which Susan Sarandon won the Oscar for Best Actress, 1995.

Vera Drake: Abortion

Vera Drake sounds like a very commonplace name. Not common, but commonplace. Vera was a popular name decades ago. One does not meet many Veras today. Drake is an archetypal British name – Sir Francis, of Armada renown, for instance. This means that the name evokes Britain in the past, a touch heroic, more than a touch commonplace. It is the perfect name for Mike Leigh's film. Vera Drake is a fiftyish, lower middle-class housewife and mother.

It is a mystery amongst observers for selection processes for the important film festivals why the 2004 Cannes Festival actually rejected *Vera Drake* for its competition. After all, Mike Leigh had had great success there with *Naked* (1993) and *All or Nothing* (2002), winning the Palme d'Or with *Secrets and Lies* (1996). Whatever the reason for the rejection, *Vera Drake* was then accepted by Venice and went on to win the Golden Lion as well as the Best Actress award for Imelda Staunton. *Vera Drake* won universal acclaim as Leigh's best film since *Secrets and Lies*. However, the headlines blared, 'Abortion film'.

There seems to be an assumption that when abortion is the theme of a film, the film is in favour of abortion. Journalists and polemicists scent the aroma of controversy and possibilities for sensational copy. In this sense, *Vera Drake* is a disappointment. The buzz about *Vera Drake* being a front-runner for the big award led to speculation about how the Catholic Church would respond. Italian journalists are said to have a reputation for being critical of the church, if not stridently anti-clerical at times, so this would provide a field day. This did not prove to be the case.

In an article in *Variety*, 19 October 2004, Gabriel Snyder wrote about marketing tactics for the movie in the US, 'Inside Move: Leigh pic plays both sides. "Vera" hoping to ride controversy to success.' His observations on what actually happened illuminate how controversy is prone to exploitation:

'With *Vera Drake*, helmer Mike Leigh may have accomplished the impossible: making a film about abortion that both sides of the debate can admire. Fine Line hopes the pic – about a homemaker and abortionist in post-war London – will be the next film to ride controversy to success, à la *The Passion of the Christ* and *Fahrenheit 9/11*. It's even enlisted pro-choice groups like NARAL… to push the pic. But so far there hasn't been any controversy. Pro-life groups, such as the U.S. Conference of Catholic Bishops, have only had positive things to say about the film. Harry Forbes, who classifies films that are considered morally offensive for the USCCB's Office of Film & Broadcast, actually gave *Vera Drake* a rave review. Noting the story doesn't "proselytize for abortion", he wrote, "Leigh's script has all the subtle nuances of 'real' people reacting to a domestic crisis." Imelda Staunton's performance, he says, "is acting of the highest order".

Forbes echoes other official Catholic voices on the film. 'Shortly after *Vera Drake* won best film honours at the Venice Film Festival, World Catholic Association for Communication proxy Peter Malone praised the film despite its subject matter. "It is not simply, or simplistically, moral judgment by unnuanced application of moral principles" …'

Snyder concludes (reminding us that his article was written two weeks before the US presidential election where pro-life and pro-choice issues were to the fore: 'In this shrill season, how refreshing.'

Two factors contribute to a more intelligent discussion of the film. First, the film itself. Mike Leigh is a master filmmaker. The second factor is Mike Leigh's own views on the theme. At his press conference in Venice, he was quick to point out that his films treat social issues but never provide 'unequivocal answers'. Leigh noted that, while we bring our own agenda to the story, we are invited to consider a wider range of perspectives. It is not simply, or simplistically, moral judgment by unnuanced application of moral principles.

Leigh said that some audiences would view Vera as a saint, committed to assisting women; others would see her as a monster, destroying lives. Some would see her prison sentence as far too harsh, while others would judge it as far too lenient: 'It's not quite about abortion as such. It's about the whole morality around us. It's an issue that's very much with us, even though abortion is legal now, and it always will be. There will always be unwanted pregnancies and disagreements on the way to deal with them. I don't deal with whether abortion is or isn't a moral thing; I'm more interested in how people deal and dealt with it. I tried to make a film about a good person criminalised.'

Most audiences hurry out as soon as final credits roll. For those who stay, they will see that Leigh dedicates his film to his parents, a doctor and a midwife.

Who is Vera Drake?

Vera Drake is a fifty-year-old housewife in North London in 1950. She is generous to a fault. Nothing is too much trouble for her. Everyone says she has a heart of gold. She is the proverbial good woman. We see her busily cleaning the homes of the wealthy, a stickler for neatness and order. We see her visiting her cantankerous and disabled mother, making sure she is comfortable and not going hungry. She has a cheerful word for everyone, including a returned soldier who leads a lonely life. She invites him round for meals. He takes a modest and quiet shine to Vera's shy and awkward daughter, eventually proposing. Her son works in a men's clothing store and has a genial patter that enables him to sell suits. (He is not above a bit of local black market dealing; Britain is not quite over the rationing and deprivations from wartime.) Her husband Stan is a quiet mechanic who works for his brother. He is also the proverbial good man, a decent man, loving father and faithful husband. The film offers us one of the most sympathetic portraits of an ordinary British working-class family. The first half of the film sets a context for a moving portrait of Vera Drake. Imelda Staunton's performance makes her memorable.

So, Leigh presents us with a very nice person. Audience judgements on her character are favourable. The audience feels that it knows and likes Vera. Without any lead in or preparation, we are shown how she performs syringe abortions for women and girls 'in need'. She has been doing this for twenty years or more. Her family know nothing about it. As with all her work, she is always chipper, her bag and syringe kit neat and functional. Everything is simple, syringe, cloth, carbolic soap. She chatters cheerfully to the girls, gently explaining to them what will happen in the miscarriage, reassuring them that everything will be all right.

By focussing on Vera herself and seeing her in action, the audience is responding on a different plane to the moral issues. This is not merely some abstract question to be answered as if it were an exam. We are privy to behaviour and motivations. We realise that only good is intended by Vera. She has been performing this help for twenty years. We hear only a few hints about her earlier story. Was abortion an issue for her own mother? Had she had an abortion when she was young? This is possible.

However, Vera has kept any information about what she does from her husband and her family. Her reference point for women 'in need' is an old school friend who takes a more business-like approach to abortion. This rather hard woman is well known as a contact for arranging abortions. She does the interviews and sets the price, pocketing it all. Vera is unaware of the money transactions. She receives nothing. It appears that she has never thought of any remuneration. She simply goes to the address provided and kindly performs her task.

Leigh has another point to make when showing us Vera's clients (which is really too strong and clinical a description of the girls and women she helps). There are frightened young girls, women who have had several abortions, a black woman without family or friends. By contrast, Leigh sketches another character with an unwanted pregnancy. She is the daughter of one of the wealthy women for whom Vera cleans house. A shy girl, she is plied with drink by a seemingly respectable young man taking her out to dinner. He rapes her. When she realises she is pregnant, she is able to get in touch with a friend (in a swanky restaurant which serves delightful afternoon teas of cakes on elegant crockery). Her road to abortion is via 'legitimate' channels, in harmony with the legislation that dates from 1866. She is interviewed by a doctor, referred to a psychiatrist who manipulates her fearful and confused answers into sounding like a threat, that this pregnancy could force her to contemplate taking her own life. At this time, this is sufficient legal grounds for a termination. The young woman is finally seen going up a hospital staircase, being reassured by the nurses that everything will go well for her.

Some reviewers were dissatisfied that this was all we saw of that character. Leigh acknowledged this but explained that it was all he wanted to show of that sub-plot: the double standards of the law and health for those who could pay while poorer women had to resort secretly, if not to backyards, then to amateur abortionists like Vera. This raises the issue of legislation concerning abortion.

One of the dilemmas facing religious people concerning moral issues like abortion or even prostitution is the distinction between the legal and the moral. A practice may be considered immoral but the question still arises as to whether the state should intervene by legislation to regulate the practice and to prevent abuses. This would make it 'legal'. St Augustine, however, is often quoted as believing that prostitution should be regulated by the state. He was obviously not condoning prostitution. Rather, he was admitting that prostitution was ingrained in society, that it could lead to all kinds of exploitation of the prostitutes, to criminal violence as well as to financial corruption by those who ran the sex industry. Several countries have enacted regulations for brothels, thus legalising prostitution without giving it moral approval. Unfortunately, some people have not been able to think through this distinction. To allow something legally does not mean that it is given moral approval.

The debates in the United States concerning the legalisation of abortion, especially at the time of presidential elections, have ensured that the discussion about the legal and moral issues of the taking of the life of the unborn remain in popular consciousness. The slogan 'Right to Life' has dominated thinking about abortion. (It has also roused such passion in some of its extreme proponents that they have felt that they must take the law into their own hands and do violence to, even kill, doctors and nurses who perform abortions.) What is not always clear in the debates and the judgements about the stances of candidates for office in the US – for example, that Senator John Kerry during the 2004 campaign should be refused communion in a Catholic church because of his allegedly being pro-abortion – is the distinction between the moral and the legal attitudes towards abortion. Someone who does not perceive abortion as immoral will have no trouble in supporting right to abortion legislation. Someone who does perceive abortion as being immoral, who is 'Pro-Life', may still vote 'Pro-Choice' in the sense that they acknowledge abortion has always been practised, despite penalties, because of the law but they believe that it is for the better good of society that this practice be regulated and supervised to avoid the ills that accompanied what were called 'backyard abortions' where money was a priority before sanitary and cleanliness issues.

By introducing the sub-plot about the wealthy girl's easy path to a legal abortion, Mike Leigh is challenging his audience to respond emotionally as well as intellectually to what Vera is doing and to think about the role of the law.

Eventually, one girl who has come with her mother for the syringing suffers severe complications and has to be taken to hospital. The mother is reluctant to give the information to the doctors concerning the contact, the payment and Vera's name. Threatened with police action, she reluctantly agrees. The hospital authorities then inform the police.

Having established the character of Vera and enabled audiences to like her as well as ponder her abortion practices for almost an hour of the film's running time, Leigh then devotes the second half of his film to Vera's arrest, interrogation, having to face her family, trial and imprisonment.

For Vera, the issues are very clear but they are only at a caring, emotional level. She has not reflected objectively on what she does. She responds to felt needs. She represents a great number of people in the Britain of that time. Legislation concerning abortion had been introduced in 1866 and had not been changed. Abortion was a criminal offence (except, as was mentioned earlier, where a termination was allowed for the sake of the psychological health of the pregnant woman). For Vera, the issue was quite simple: even though the law forbade what she was doing, she was responding to a felt need. In Leigh's screenplay, there is no religious context for 1950s Britain. The Drake family's values are traditional rather than religious. The abortion issue for Vera is a secular issue not a religiously moral one. There is no church context, no theoretical moral or ethical context, simply people working on personal instincts and their own moral sense for values and action. There were personal criteria for some, objective criteria for others: a tradition of abortion practices and a tradition of legislation against abortion.

Since the change of legislation in the 1960s, with the performing of abortions in hospitals and clinics not being legally criminal acts, 'pro-life' has become more than merely a moral theological campaign (which it is) but it has also become a political cause. History reminds us that when an ethical issue moves beyond the realm of values and morals to the political arena, some single-minded adherents fight for a cause rather than the issue itself. Sometimes, for what they consider a higher good, they adopt some of the attitudes they are fighting against. Hatred rather than right reason takes over and sometimes extremist behaviour (even to killing of opponents) characterises and then gives a bad name to the cause. We have seen allegedly devout Christians so consumed by their cause that they take life into their own hands to prevent (and avenge?) the taking of the life of the unborn.

Mike Leigh takes a very different approach to his controversial material. In the second part of the film, Vera is arrested and questioned. She is shocked and shamed. She is forced to think about her actions from a different perspective from her kind helping out of the women. Whatever stance the audience may have towards abortion, audience empathy with Vera makes us share her bewilderment at the implications of what she has done and how other people see it. There is her dismay at the girl who has suffered medical complications from the procedure and who could have died had she not been taken at once to hospital. For Vera, it becomes a more serious problem and makes her face the reality of loss of life, of taking life.

The methods that Mike Leigh uses for creating his screenplays are well known. He invites his cast to long improvisation sessions. However, he does not let the cast know the full outline of his story. Rather, he reveals pieces to each of them on what he considers a need to know basis. Having provided a context for a scene or an episode, he encourages them to be creative in their interpretation of the situation. When he has found a satisfying interpretation and performance, he writes a meticulous script which the actors enact quite exactly. They contribute to the development of the screenplay and Leigh writes it.

This leads to effective dramatic tensions in the film. In the second half, we see the members of the family reacting quite differently. The son, for instance, is horrified at what his mother has been doing. He cannot understand it. He does not approve it. He does not know how to deal with it – nor how to deal with his mother. This is especially demanding for him when she is allowed out on bail and the family gathers to celebrate Christmas. Through this character and his reaction (which is alarming, but understandable, when he cannot be compassionate towards his mother), Leigh has introduced the traditional stance against abortion for our reflection. Perhaps more challenging is the quiet attitude of Vera's husband, Stanley. He is an ordinary, uncomplicated man who has seen terrible war action and suffering. He has been brought up to consider abortion as outside the law and, therefore, immoral. But he experiences the shock of learning that the wife he has loved for such a long time has been doing something that he has disapproved of. He is the embodiment of the old adage of hating the sin but loving the sinner.

It is Vera's daughter's fiancé, the lonely man that has

been made to feel at home in the Drake household, who voices the sympathetic and supportive attitudes to Vera. He does not focus on the death of the unborn. Rather, he makes the comment on the kind of world a child who has been deemed unwanted comes into, whether the child could be loved and grow up in a healthy way.

These are not ultimate rational arguments. However, as in all good case studies, they present the different points of view in the context of personal lives and decisions rather than as abstract test questions.

This comes finally into focus in the trial sequences where, according to the legislation of the times, Vera has to give an account of what she has done, where doctors and police speak about the medical and legal aspects of the case. In putting forward a witness to Vera as a good person, the issues of intention, of exploitation and remuneration (which are alien to her approach), of the plight of the women wanting abortions are all voiced.

It is in the light of the range of elements brought out in the trial and of the then legislation, that sentence is given. Vera, as a good woman, dreads gaol. However, she accepts her sentence. It is too severe for those who sympathise with what she has done, too lenient for those who are dismayed by the taking of unborn life. Leigh sends us out from his film without an equivocal answer but with story, characters, moral dilemmas, different stances voiced for us to sharpen our moral senses no matter what our approach to abortion is. He does, however, put a final image for our consideration. Vera, whom we know well, meets other abortionists in prison, hard women with longer sentences whose concern is money rather than the value of human life be it that of the mother or the unborn child.

The difficulty with labelling a film 'about abortion' is that this merely tells us the subject, or one of the subjects, of the film. The Biblical story of David and Bathsheba is about adultery and murder but that is merely a labelling description. What we need to know is 'how' these issues are presented.

This is the criterion for a moral evaluation of a film. This means, as a correspondent for Vatican Radio was reported as saying on air during the Venice Festival, that Leigh's film is 'difficult and interesting' and 'avoided propaganda and tentative and facile conclusions'. As has been already noted, best pastoral practice has urged Christians to compassion and forgiveness (to the extent of 'seventy times seven') to condemn the sin but not the sinner. Leigh's portrait of Vera Drake contributes to that way of looking at her despite what she does.

'The seamless garment of life' indicates that any taking of life, from the unborn, to the enemy, to the evil criminal, is not the Gospel ideal. One of the quandaries for many sincere people today is coping with the sometime ease with which those in favour of abortion speak about the unborn child (preferring the language of embryo, foetus rather than child) and then campaign for animal rights with such passion or argue against the harm caused by passive smoking. One of the greatest challenges from life issues is that of a coherent and consistent morality.

Physical and sexual abuse of the young

In terms of the quality of life and the seamless garment of life, one of the greatest threats is abuse of the young. Not only has it been a horrendous revelation over the last twenty years – even more so during the last ten – that adults at home, in institutions and in organised rings have been physically and sexually assaulting children, but that members of Churches and an alarmingly high number of clergy and members of religious orders have been accused of this kind of activity and have been found guilty in courts and have been gaoled.

Until the 1980s, most people did not think of going to the police to press criminal charges. There were very few precedents. We are learning now that concerned parents did go to ecclesiastical authorities but that there was a lack of awareness about how serious the matters really were; that there were no protocols to guide church leaders in how to deal with clergy misconduct of this nature; that there was an immediate concern for the welfare of the accused rather than concern and compassion for the complainants and a belated switch to language of victims and perpetrators. The behaviour was secret, hidden, smoothed over with lying deception by perpetrators, the exercise of emotional blackmail and the reinforcing of guilt feelings in the victims. While errant clergy were moved from place to place to avoid scandal without the realisation that they would offend again, or were sent to institutes for therapy, there was little help, counselling or compensation for the victims. In fact, worldwide, secular and church authorities are still trying to grapple with psychological understanding of the mind and emotions of an abuser. Again, worldwide, many secular and ecclesiastical authorities have not yet come to grips with the appropriate protocols of how to deal with cases morally and legally.

Some dioceses and religious orders, especially in English-speaking countries like Canada, Australia, Britain and Ireland, have taken very serious steps to do the right thing for victims and to deal honestly and justly with perpetrators. However, the US experience of 2002 which led to so many victims making accusations with the consequent financial compensatory claims that have bankrupted several dioceses, has a continued impact in so many dimensions of church life: the role of the priest, the psychological and emotional health and maturity of men and women in responsible ecclesiastical roles, the erosion of trust by the faithful, the enormous anger and resentment, the long-term ill effects of abuse on the victims. Belatedly, revelations have emerged from continental European countries. Many are waiting for scandals to be revealed in Asia and Africa.

News headlines have not been reticent about the Church. While focussing on Church personnel being abusers – and one must, because, along with parents and teachers, they are the people who should be above suspicion and should be the most trustworthy – the cases against workers in child-care institutions and schools have been frighteningly numerous.

There have been a number of movies dramatising this theme. As early as 1990, HBO produced a telemovie on the first reported case of abuse of a boy in Louisiana in the mid-1980s. It was called *Judgment*. Keith Carradine and Blythe Danner starred as the parents of the boy and David Strathairn was the priest in question. It was strong and surprising drama at the time, especially in its portrayal of the Bishop and his Vicar General and their handling of the case, their juridical issues and the pastoral issues.

In more recent years, there have been some very strong films. Ireland's *Song for a Raggy Boy* (2003) shows physical and sexual abuse of boys in an Irish school of the 1930s. *The Magdalene Sisters* (Golden Lion winner at Venice, 2002) portrayed life within a Dublin institution for girls and women considered as misbehaving sexually, a laundry run by severe nuns on behalf of the state. Pedro Almodóvar's *La Mala educación* had a particularly Spanish perspective, indicating the emotions of the abusing priest as well as the aftermath for the victim.

There have also been several films that have nothing to do with the Church, Todd Solontz's *Happiness* (1999) was a strong film on a range of sexual issues including a father who was an abuser. Tim Robbins won a Best Supporting Actor Oscar for portraying a man severely affected from the abuse by some strangers in Clint Eastwood's *Mystic River* (2003). *The Woodsman* (2004) starred Kevin Bacon as an abuser of young girls emerging from gaol after serving his sentence.

The case study for this chapter is a secular rather than a Church-related story. It means looking at paedophilia in the ordinary context of a small town and of day-by-day life rather than a story that carries the extra baggage of a clerical offender. By looking at a secular case study first, one has a stronger awareness of the enormity of abuse by a religious person.

Mysterious Skin

Mysterious Skin (2004) is a surprising film from writer-director, Gregg Araki. For more than a decade Araki has produced many B-budget films like *Splendour, Nowhere, The Doom Generation, The Living End*. His films were noted for sexual themes, drug taking. He also highlighted homosexual themes in many of his stories. They were rough, full of coarse language, rough and ready in both form and content.

With *Mysterious Skin*, he has adapted a novel by Scott Heim. The novel came out in 1995 when charges were beginning to surface in various organisations. This film focuses on families and the paedophile is the baseball coach. The setting is the late 1980s, early 1990s.

The film is strong in its portrayal of sexual abuse. However, Araki keeps a balance between being prurient and showing the dramatic and dire impact of sexual abuse. While some audiences may find it disturbing, it is a necessary disturbance, learning to understand the reality of paedophilia, the psychology of the abuser, the long-lasting effects of the experience on the abused. In fact, the film is visually reticent, the directness being restricted to verbal frankness – which is much easier to absorb than visual explicitness.

The film focuses on two very different boys. As teenagers they are portrayed by Joseph Gordon Levitt and by Brady Corbett. Levitt portrays a young hustler. Corbett portrays an introverted young man who has no memory of being abused, no idea that he has been abused. He has so successfully created a psychological block that, when he sees a television program about UFOs, he begins to think that the missing hours of his life that he has no way of accounting for were caused by his being abducted by aliens. By the end of the film, when the two adolescents come together, they go to the house where the abuse took place and the hustler explains to the innocent boy what actually took place. This is a harrowing experience as the young man realises what has happened to him, the memories come back. This is the moment when the film ends, leaving the future for the two boys and a sense of wonder and anticipation as well as alarm for the audience.

The film also has a good supporting cast with Michelle Trachtenberg (Harriet the Spy, television's Buffy the Vampire Slayer) as the best friend of the hustler. Jeff Licon is a good friend to both of the boys. Bill Sage does well in the unenviable role of the coach. Elizabeth Shue appears as the mother of the hustler while Lisa Long and Chris Malkey are the parents of the disturbed boy. Billy Drago and Richard Riehl appear as clients of the hustler.

The film is disturbing almost from its beginning. The initial focus is on Neil, speaking in voiceover and commenting on his attraction for the baseball coach and hinting at the implications of this. However, it is the pre-pubescent Neil who is speaking in this way. And this is already shocking in its way. However, Araki (who can empathise with the characters because of his own orientation) is suggesting that for some youngsters, their sexual focus emerges at a young age. This does not necessarily lead to abuse but that in this period where so much attention has to be on victims, there may be some deep level response to the sexuality but not to elicit abuse. This is an area that has not received a great deal of attention. In this screenplay, it emerges that Neil has been complicit in the sexual behaviour. He has also been seduced into being an ally of the abuser in his activities with other boys. This compounds the evil compulsions of the perpetrator, the abuse of a child and the contamination of another child into being an abuser.

This is a very delicate issue and needs a great deal more research and reflection, an issue that will continue to be a source for study well after the myriad cases that are being brought to light have been examined.

Neil talks about his orientation. He indicates what happened during his visits to the coach's house. Much of this is visualised in the early part of the film – the more seductive aspects rather than sexual activity. While the audience tries to grapple with understanding the mentality of the young boy, the screenplay portrays the coach as a complex, naïve but knowing seducer, who uses the language of games and seeming innocence, who is really an emotionally and morally immature boy. This is one of the themes of several films on this topic. In *Bump in the Night* (1991), Christopher Reeve portrays a university lecturer in literature who can relate (with superficial depth) only to a young boy whom he abducts, takes on outings to the zoo. It is on this basis that the abusive sexual compulsions build up. Pedro Almodóvar creates a powerful scene in *La Mala educación* where the priest rector of the school sits in rapt attention at the community dinner table while the 10-year-old boy with whom he is infatuated sings a song for his birthday. Alarm and disgust at the paedophiles has obscured the need (certainly in the media and other public arenas) for trying to understand the mentality of the emotionally stunted abusers, their attractions and their exploitations.

As with the boy in *La Mala educación*, Neil is knowing and becomes a male hustler in the town. Neil hangs out with his friends, gay adolescent, Eric, and his best friend from school days, Wendy. They follow Neil around, help him with pick-ups, are not above some violent mischief. When Wendy moves to New York city, Neil later follows, trying to get a job, but falling foul of some violent and vicious clients. His mother, a single mother with a number of men friends, has no idea of her son's behaviour around town, let alone his inner life.

The early part of the film also deals with Brian. He has no voiceover. We simply see that he is an awkward, bookish, bespectacled child who is urged to join the baseball team – with little success on the pitch though cared for by the coach. We see that one day, his parents find him in the cellar in a state of shock. He has lost five hours and can give no explanation of what has happened to him. This mystery is not explained until the end of the film.

Brian comes from your average American home – although the father eventually walks out on his family. Brian loves his mother, his sister. He does well at school. He is befriended by Eric at school who leads him astray only by trying alcohol. When he sees a television programme about UFOs and the testimony of a girl from a neighbouring town who was abducted and recounts the treatment she received from the aliens, he goes to see her and becomes persuaded that this is what happened to him in those mysterious five hours. They get along well. Later when she comes to visit him, she makes a sexual advance and he recoils and goes back into his shell. This indicates some fear of sexuality but Brian has no idea why. The abuse he experienced has no conscious effect on him. Rather, it has closed him down unawares, setting up intimacy barriers, creating an atmosphere of fear.

Mysterious Skin does not purport to probe all aspects of abuse. Rather, in focussing on the two boys, it shows one who is conscious of what happened to him, his part in it and the consequences, the other who is oblivious but knows there is something wrong with him.

By the climax of the film, the story of the film, the two case studies we have been offered for our reflection, have led us into this generally unwelcome area of abuse. Our attitudes have been tested, our sympathies with the victims and antipathies towards the perpetrators have been made more emotionally explicit. We are probably bewildered by many facets. But this has all been preparation for the final revelation.

Eric introduces Brian to Neil. Brian feels that there is some connection between them. Neil decides to take Brian to the coach's house, into the room where the abuse took place. The audience is now further shocked as they listen to Neil's story. It was he who abused the victims like Brian along with the coach, not once but many times. He pimped for the coach. He assisted the coach. He eventually explains to Brian what happened on the mysterious day, how, after the session, the coach and Neil took the traumatised Brian back to his home and left him in the cellar for his parents to find.

Painful as this is for Brian, it is important that the reality be brought to his consciousness and that he owns it. He needs to move towards acceptance of this reality, towards some kind of peace which may include forgiving Neil and, if possible, some forgiveness of the coach so that he can live his life in freedom. For Neil, the confession in itself as well as to Brian, may bring about some honesty and feeling for himself.

Sexual abuse has been one of the greatest threats to tear apart the seamless garment of life for the victims who are, we realise, far more numerous than we would have dared to imagine only a generation earlier. *Mysterious Skin* is a mature attempt to bring the issue to worldwide screen consciousness. After a long apprenticeship in his own almost private kind of films, Araki has made a significant contribution to American movies and to an exploration of serious themes.

Capital punishment

The evocative title of the 1958 film which gave Susan Hayward her Best Actress Oscar for portraying executed criminal, Barbara Graham, was *I Want to Live*. If any phrase summarises the basic human drive to be a person with quality of life, it is 'I want to live'.

Thomas Aquinas, the thirteenth-century philosopher and theologian, noted that there were four basic human drives. They can be briefly summarised as the drives to be, to live, to live in society and to move towards the transcendent (for which he added, as the theologian he was, 'what we call God'). These are the basic values that form the core of any ethical and moral discussion between believers of all faiths and between believers and non-believers. The image of the seamless garment of life includes all these facets but, with the emphasis on the quality of life, it denotes the full meaning of 'I want to live'.

The two principal threats to the quality of life are the betrayal/abuse of sexuality and violence. The next case study is concerned with violence. It needs to be said that violence is a very ambiguous word. In more recent times, it is the blanket word to cover all the presentations in the media and the arts to describe what is considered offensively disruptive in papers and magazines, films, in television, in computer games. Violence is a bad thing.

This does not deal adequately with distinctions that need to be made when considering 'violence' in real life as well as mediated violence. It should be noted at once that we are talking about any aggression, whether active or passive, that threatens or attacks in any physical, emotional or psychological way. This can also be called 'violation'. The difficulty is that there are times when someone has to use some form of violence appropriately. To save a person unaware of an oncoming vehicle from being knocked down, someone might push them – hard – out of harm's way. What of self-defence? What of protecting someone from aggression? What of resistance to tyranny? This is a continuing vexed issue. This latter issue is explored in a Gospel context in Martin Dobermeier's striking documentary feature, *Bonhoeffer*. It shows how the theologian who believed in 'the cost of discipleship', in living up to the ideals of the Sermon on the Mount, and was led to pacifist stances, also became involved in the plot to kill Hitler, was arrested and finally executed in Dachau. The disapproval of violence cannot be merely simplistic.

Linguistically, it is awkward and would not work in practice, but one could say that what threatens the quality of life is 'undue' violence. This would mean that there is acceptable violence or 'due' violence. But it is hard to imagine this kind of distinction being readily taken up and used in discussions or conversations. The reality, however, is important: there can be situations where violence is appropriate and situations where it is not appropriate, due and undue violence.

A word that suggests itself in connection with undue violence and which is often used in common vocabulary is 'brutality'. There is never any justification for brutality. It is not appropriate in the home, in the schoolyard, in the workplace, in offices of government or Church. Any genocide is brutality writ large. Pictures of American soldiers torturing

Iraqi prisoners (physically, emotionally and psychologically) are pictures of brutality. They led to courts martial and convictions. Popular movies and computer games that indulge in vicarious killings and relish the techniques of destroying opponents, stacking up high body counts are not just portraying violence. What they show (and what they indicate in the mind and imagination behind them) is brutality.

During the Sermon on the Mount, Jesus reminded his listeners (after saying Blessed are the poor in spirit, the meek, the merciful, the pure in heart...) that in olden times it was said, 'an eye for an eye, a tooth for a tooth'. Now he wants to tell them that this hallowed Lex Talionis, Law of Vengeance, was old hat, was obsolete, that it belonged to barbaric times when people were hard of heart and could interpret justice only in this way. To the disbelief of his listeners (not just at the Sermon but right throughout the ages until now), he urged the turning of one's other cheek to be struck again by an assailant. This is the advice that draws on the nobility of the human spirit rather than satisfying blood lust. Maybe blood lust is overstating an attitude towards capital punishment but look at the crowds in London who went out to see a hanging, drawing and quartering. In fact, Mel Gibson portrayed them vividly at the death of William Wallace at the end of *Braveheart*. Of course, he showed it even more graphically (with some who found the film distasteful wondering whether he was not indulging it) in the death of the man who spoke the Sermon on the Mount, Jesus' suffering in *The Passion of the Christ*.

This leads us more directly to our third case study on the seamless garment of life, a case study on the ending of life, capital punishment. It raises the question whether capital punishment is brutal and whether a society that executes its criminals is brutal.

Dead Man Walking

Sister Helen Prejean, an American Sister of St Joseph working in Louisiana, would never have dreamed when she made her vows as a nun (which we can see in the flashback footage of ceremonies used at the opening of *Dead Man Walking*) that she would have become something of a household name forty years later. Her prison ministry, through her campaigning, her articles and books, the documentaries, the feature film and the opera, became widely known in the mid 1990s and has given encouragement and hope to those facing the issues of capital punishment. At the Oscar ceremony in April 1996, she sat in the front row of the theatre beside Susan Sarandon, watched worldwide by millions as the actress paid tribute to the nun in her Oscar acceptance speech.

In adapting Helen Prejean's book, Tim Robbins combined stories of two prisoners on death row into the character of Matthew Poncelet (played convincingly by Sean Penn). Poncelet writes to Sr Helen who is teaching underprivileged children and asks her to be his spiritual director in the weeks before his execution. When she goes to visit him, not knowing what to expect, she is caught up in the Gospel teachings of forgiveness of sinners (seven times seventy) and the image of Jesus on the cross pardoning the repentant thief and promising him paradise that day. The priest chaplain is not impressed, preferring to tick her off on the issue of whether she is wearing a traditional nun's habit or not. Her community, however, are supportive, even being prepared to make available one of the order's plots for Poncelet to be buried in. The sisters also join in protests against capital punishment as does the local bishop.

Her ministry leads her in two directions. She is first drawn to the spiritual accompaniment of the prisoners. Whatever they have done, they have the right to pardon by God and to trying to repair in some ways the brutality they have perpetrated. This is a ministry of discernment. Sr Helen has to listen attentively to the words and to the heart of Matthew

Poncelet. If she is to succeed in bringing any quality into the final part of his life, she has to be a catalyst for grace. He has to acknowledge truly and profoundly what he has done, the cruelty towards his victims which, in his case, are both the violation of rape and the ultimate violation of life in murder. She has to foster his sense of repentance, of sorrow, of the need for some kind of confession, of absolution from God, from her, from his victims and from their families, for some kind of atonement and reconciliation.

Dramatically speaking, Tim Robbins has made a judicious decision to include the flashbacks to the actual crime at this point of the film. They become part of Poncelet's confession. As we see what he did, we know that he is truly remembering and acknowledging the profound and careless evil of what he has done. It is visually shocking (and earned the film more restrictive classifications than it might otherwise have received). Confession is not merely a matter of words (which are always easier to hear than the visual impact of seeing crimes like these in action). For Poncelet, this confession to Sr Helen is a conversion in the best sense. Profound sin can be described as an 'aversion' from right and good and from God. It is a complete aversion, a turning away. Profound repentance can be described, therefore, as a 'conversion' to right and good and to God. It is a complete conversion, a turning towards. (If we want a film to explore the deeper implications of the Church's sacrament of Penance, *Dead Man Walking* is a fine suggestion.)

Ultimately, Matthew Poncelet does confess to her and if ever there was a cinema moment when the giving of sacramental absolution by any minister, irrespective of whether that person be a priest or not cried out for blessing, this is it. Yet, as a nun, all she can offer is prayerful forgiveness. Even state rules forbid her to include any hymns in these final prayers before execution because the music could stir an emotional response that would be detrimental to the execution processes. When Sr Helen sings one of the hymns by the St Louis Jesuits, well known to so many

Catholics, it is a scene of love and reconciliation, of courage in faith before death. She tells him to look at her because she will be for him the face of love as he dies.

Dead Man Walking uses a dramatic device to open its audiences' eyes to look further than Matthew Poncelet. Sr Helen's eyes are opened in an unexpectedly emotional way. While we are shown the grief of the Poncelet family, especially Matthew's mother and what the shame of the crime and the pain of the execution mean to her, the screenplay at first gives minimum attention to the families of the victims. It is only when Sr Helen goes to see them out of courtesy that she is made to realise that she has neglected her ministry to the survivors of Poncelet's crimes. They assume that, especially as a nun, she has come to comfort them, to be on their side. The Percy's are angry with her, accuse her of arrogance and order her to leave their house. So far, the audience has been caught up in her prison ministry and the good she could do for the prisoners. We have overlooked the families, just as she has. The scenes of her dealing with the families, their disillusionment when they judge that she is ministering to 'the enemy' are harrowing for her and for those in the audience who realise that crime affects more than the immediate victims and the perpetrators. Her horizons, and ours, have to widen. Even more demands are made on compassion.

This plot thread comes to its climax when members of the victims' families attend the execution. They have not been able to gain the same perspective as Sr Helen. Perhaps their feelings for vengeance have been tempered to feelings for justice. Poncelet attempts to convey something of his repentance and need for their forgiveness but they have not reached that point. Before he is strapped, Poncelet extends his arms in the form of a cross. We are reminded of Calvary, that Jesus gave his life on the cross for all – including the repentant thief.

What is significant and is something that gives the film an even greater spiritual depth as well as challenge to the audience is the final sequence. The camera tracks outside a church. As we look in, we see Sr Helen and Mr Delacroix, the father of the boy (who has listened to Sr Helen but has not been able to bring himself to forgive, who has attended the execution) both kneeling in prayer. If the final virtue in the seamless garment of life is reconciliation between those who have been enemies, which leads towards peace, then this is a perfect ending to this film.

Quality of life, capital punishment?

In the meantime, Sr Helen's ministry continues. The second path on which she was led is that of the reconsideration of the place of capital punishment in modern, 'civilised' society.

During the twentieth century, many countries abolished the death penalty. The century saw many genocides, not simply the execution of a criminal whose sentence was intended as an appropriate retribution for crimes committed, but the execution of millions of innocent men, women and children. Ethnic discrimination (and the ironic title, 'ethnic cleansing') because of race, religious persecution, fundamentalist fanaticism, we have witnessed it all: Armenians in the early twentieth century, the Holocaust of six million Jews and the concentration camp and prisoner of war camps, the marginalised, the Soviet Gulags, Hutus versus Tutsis and devastation and murder in the Sudan. We might have thought that by the beginning of the twenty-first century, the human race would have been able to think less of imposing death and more of improving and rehabilitating life.

Opponents of the death penalty raise issues of miscarriages of justice, the execution of the innocent. How many innocent people need to be hanged or gassed or poisoned before it is enough. Surely, one; only one? There have been many films made about Joan of Arc. A religious woman (and since 1920 a canonised saint), she received the death penalty. Her capital punishment by burning was particularly cruel. She was considered a witch. Arthur Miller's celebrated play, *The*

Crucible (and the 1996 film version with Daniel Day Lewis), reminds us that even righteous (and, of course, self-righteous) men and women can execute their neighbours because of prejudice and fear as well as malice and greed.

Since the death penalty has been an important issue in the United States, especially in the States of Texas and Florida, where the President of the US and his brother have been governors and have a high statistical record of executions, the rest of the world has been very conscious of it. With the 2003-04 abduction of citizens from many nations contributing to the re-building of Iraq (ten Nepalese workers for instance, as well as higher-profiled citizens from the US, Britain, Japan, Italy…) and the release on video of some of the lead-up to the executions as well as the graphic deaths, one would hope that there is a greater alertness and sensitivity towards the atrocity of execution.

A wall graffiti of the mid-1960s read, "The quality of a society can be gauged by its treatment of prisoners".

This is the journey made by Sr Helen Prejean and many of the activists against capital punishment. *Dead Man Walking* shows her venturing into the previously unknown world of prisons, her meeting with humane officials, her meeting with those whose attitudes towards the prisoners were unforgiving and sometimes brutal. This led her to protests and demonstrations, letter-writing and picketing. The screenplay is fair in presenting intellectual, emotional and justice/retribution/deterrent arguments for the death penalty as well as intellectual, emotional, human dignity/rehabilitation arguments against. Crowds are outside the prison, taking opposite stances. And the challenge for the audience is where do you stand – and why?

Since the 1950s, there have been some novels and films that have had quite a high profile raising issues of the death penalty. *I Want to Live* was strong stuff, black and white realism, in 1958 (less persuasive in the telemovie remake of 1983, still powerful but in technicolor and looking bright and glossy). Truman Capote wrote an analysis of the criminal mentality, especially of two individuals who might not have committed murder but who, working together, found a lethal co-dependent evil and brutality. *In Cold Blood*, Richard Brooks 1968 austere and metallic-black-and-white film version is well worth seeing to try to understand the mentalities of crime and punishment. (Once again, the telemovie version of 1996 is more glossy.) Novelist Norman Mailer wrote about the execution of Gary Gilmore in *The Executioner's Song* (also filmed for television in 1982).

Two other films are worth noting on this topic. The telemovie, *The Execution of Raymond Graham* (1985), with Jeff Fahey as the condemned criminal and Morgan Freeman as the warden, like *Dead Man Walking*, takes us through the process for and against execution, shows us the criminal, his guilt, some extenuating circumstances, the unforgiving families, especially the father, played by Josef Sommer who attends the execution by lethal injection and discovers how it affects him. Because it was made for the television audience, its treatment of its themes is less harrowing than films made for the big screen.

One of the films on capital punishment made for the big screen at the same time as *Dead Man Walking* but quite overshadowed by it was Bruce Beresford's *Last Dance,* with Sharon Stone as a criminal on death row. Stone gives a tough performance as a woman who has had a harsh life, whose destiny may have inevitably been the gas chamber. The film shows her case being taken up by a young, sincere but inexperienced lawyer (Rob Morrow). All of these films have execution scenes. Popular reaction tends to be 'I really don't want to watch things like that'. If it is too much for the screen, then should it happen in real life?

Life

Vera Drake, Mysterious Skin and *Dead Man Walking* are more powerful than any sermon on the quality of life. Cardinal Bernardin's image of the seamless garment will not persuade everyone. On the other hand, it reminds us that our attitudes towards life should be authentic and consistent. Life is to be protected from its inception. Life is not to be betrayed or abused. Life is to be treated with dignity at its end, even for those who have forfeited their freedom because of crime, because of some brutality and violation against fellow human beings.

Life issues are always open to debate because we do not live by abstract principles alone. Film case studies offer an opportunity for ordinary people as well as legal, ethical and theological academics to participate in the debates because they have responded to the stories.

CHAPTER 3

Who Says We Don't Need Another Hero?

Back in the days when Mel Gibson was simply Mad Max, before he became lethal weapon, Martin Riggs, Tina Turner travelled to Australia to appear with him in *Mad Max Beyond Thunderdome*. Her theme song for the movie was 'We don't need another hero'. This was more than a touch ironic because that is precisely what this group of nomads, stranded in the desert, did need: Max the hero. It was, as a *Newsweek* sub-editor wrote, the time of 'Apocalypse Pow'!

With compliments to *Newsweek* for this phrase, we might say that it is always a time of Apocalypse Pow – and never more so than in time beyond time: in screen time. Tina has been proven absolutely wrong over the last twenty years. It is always time for a hero. During the summer months of blockbuster movie releases, we seem to need a new hero every other week. In 2004, from May to August, there was a succession of heroes: *Van Helsing, Troy, The Day After Tomorrow, Spiderman 2, Catwoman, I Robot, The Bourne Identity, Alien versus Predator* (like the earlier Freddy versus Jason, a 'hero' who is the lesser of two evils)… and there was the welcome reappearance of Shrek, along with the captivating Puss in Boots!

With *The Revenge of the Sith* in 2005, George Lucas brought to a conclusion his Star Wars epic. Episode III explained how the hero Annakin sold himself to the Dark Side and was transformed into Darth Vader. The conclusion of this episode, however, leads us back to the beginning of the original Star Wars and the birth of the hero and heroine of the Galaxy, Luke Skywalker and Princess Leia.

In an era where the old certainties seem to be disappearing too fast, with only a kind of post-modern cleveristic relativism taking its place, people are left bewildered. In our heart of hearts we want a world of values. But, these days, what are the real values? The twenty-first century began with the Al Qaeda attack on the World Trade Centre in New York and the Pentagon in Washington. As the twentieth century ended, there was a Gulf War against Saddam Hussein, there was genocide in Rwanda, internecine wars in the Balkans, the bombing of Serbia and Kosovo, Chechen uprisings against Russia, the bombing of US embassies in Kenya and Tanzania. With September 11, 2001, the unthinkable happened. The seemingly impregnable United States became not only a casualty of terrorism, but a major target of terrorism. With the immediate bombing of Afghanistan after 9/11, the build-up to the war against Saddam Hussein and the war in Iraq, with division of opinion about the legitimacy of the war vis-à-vis the United Nations and its resolutions, followed by the insurgency against the coalition in Iraq (with the revelations about American military torturing and degrading prisoners), terrorist bombings in Mombassa, Bali and Madrid, where can we rediscover the certainties?

A symptom of this apprehensiveness was the extraordinary box-office and critical success of Michael Moore's *Fahrenheit 9/11*. If only half of what Moore included in his clever and unashamedly partisan polemic against the Bush administration is authentic, then that is still truly alarming. Not the threats from outside the US, but the stances and behaviour of the American government itself. *Fahrenheit 9/11* made US$120,000,000 in the United States alone during from June to August 2004. That suggests that more than 12,000,000 Americans went to see it within ten weeks – and in an election year where, by the time of the nomination conventions, polls suggested that the candidates were running neck and neck.

These are world perspectives, perspectives on societies as a whole, perspectives on violence, aggression and the exercise of power and control. On the level of corporate morality, exposé and court cases concern global companies, their bankruptcies, their misinformation, their being organisations of greed and mismanagement of assets: Enron, Shell, Halliburton... The twenty-first century opened with famines in Africa, atrocities in the Sudan, drug dealers from South America to Afghanistan exploiting addictions, viruses spread through the worldwide web... Where are our values?

On the more personal and family level, we have discovered violent and sexual abuse within families and abuse perpetrated by respected members of society and of the churches. Life issues are unresolved as debates and demonstrations continue on the taking of life, whether in the womb or by capital punishment. Fidelity issues have repercussions in casual relationships, in family break-up and its consequences for children who need stability for their growth and maturity.

Enough of our woes. Every period has commentators who lament that the world has reached its lowest ebb. We are living, so it seems to us, the worst. But any glance back into history will reveal that times past could be just as dire as the circumstances of today.

One of the main sources for certainties and values was religion. While Christians number millions, church attendance in many countries is diminishing, especially among the young who are the churches' future, many take refuge in the rigid certainties proposed by more fundamentalist churches, setting up protective boundaries, especially in doctrinal orthodoxy and in matters of sexuality (less so in concerns of violence). Church leaders like John Paul II have been significant examples of witness to the Gospel on a world level. But, these days, leaders have to be seen to earn the right to be followed and what they say has to be credible. This is not always the case. A leader has to be charismatic, especially on television, and body language and sound bytes have to appear, at least, as genuine.

World religions are at a crossroads, especially as they come under the scrutiny of men and women all over the world – and, with Internet connections, instantly. As with Christianity, religion and politics are intermingled whether they should be or not. Recent years have seen the prominence of Islam on the world stage with the danger that the simplistic interpretation of Islam – that it is monolithic – will be used in bigoted and aggressive ways. Judaism carries the burden of struggle in the history of Israel and the Palestinian uprisings. India has seen persecutions of as well as by Hindus. The major world religion that has the best press now is Buddhism. People are attracted by its contemplation, its selfless rituals and its preaching of non-violence.

It is a big a step from the desire for certainties while they do not seem to be evident – to reflecting on movie heroes. But we shall take it.

Screen heroes

Of course, movie heroes, especially those who derive from comic books and comic strips, inhabit a world of fantasy. We take refuge in this world of fantasy and one danger is to remain there and to believe it is real. This is what some children do at different stages of their lives. To stay in the fantasy world (with all respect to 'Trekkies' and Star Wars devotees) is childish. No growth or maturity.

However, screen heroes can be signs of hope, symbols of the struggle between good and evil, encouragement to move away from attitudes of selfishness, to identify values, especially those of justice, and to become more active, more engaged in life. Many commentators see them as role models. After all, these heroes are seen by millions of people around the world and at almost the same time. Mass role models! This is global and mass communication through entertainment and through values challenge. Some commentators lament that the screen has become a substitute for the altar and the pulpit, that so many people have their values strengthened by seeing these movies rather than by attending church or listening to a sermon. This, of course, is a challenge to the art of preaching in an audiovisual age, where words do not stand alone, where they are accompanied by images and require a different art of attention, emotional response and understanding.

When did this all begin?

Since the movies began, especially in the United States, there were cowboys. During the 1940s and 1950s, there was John Wayne opening up the West and winning the war. By the middle of the 1950s, Charlton Heston was giving audiences *The Ten Commandments* (and who, of a certain age, does not imagine Moses looking like Charlton Heston?). He went on to be Ben Hur, El Cid, General Gordon and the survivor of *The Planet of the Apes*. But, it was not easy to be a hero in the 1960s. Clint Eastwood was 'The Man With No Name' with a fistful of dollars and a few dollars more. The times (and most other things, including the churches and government) were a-changing. Drug culture, the pill, hippies, Vietnam. Look at most of the Oscar-winning films from 1967 to 1975: *In the Heat of the Night, Midnight Cowboy, Patton, The French Connection, The Godfather, Godfather II, One Flew Over the Cuckoo's Nest* (omitting some relief in 1968 with *Oliver* and 1973 with *The Sting*). The American president who went into the White House at the beginning of 1961 with the image of Camelot, John F. Kennedy, was assassinated within three years. His rival at the time, Richard Nixon, won the presidency in 1968 but had to resign in shame in 1974. Not an era of screen heroes.

But, in the 1970s, enough may have been enough. Saigon fell in April 1975 and the United States experienced post-war traumatic stress. Fortunately for morale, 1976 was the bicentenary of American independence. It was an election year and Jimmy Carter (who did not get a second term, but is still active as a decent diplomat in his eighties) became president. And the Oscar… goes to *Rocky*. Sylvester Stallone's creation, Rocky Balboa (the original film and four sequels) brought the hero back to the screen. America and the world loved him. Rocky was poor. Rocky was the underdog. Rocky was a family man. Rocky had ambitions. Rocky was tough and trained vigorously. Rocky was tempted by false riches and glory. Rocky resisted. Rocky triumphed. And we can see Rocky jogging up the steps of that monument in Philadelphia, the city of brotherly love where two hundred years earlier the Declaration of Independence was signed. Bill Conti's score and theme from the film became an immediate evocation of guts and victory.

Maybe after Rocky, Tina Turner could have been right. There seemed to be no need for another hero. But there was one on the way, a hero not just for Americans, but a hero for the whole world, for the galaxies.

Star Wars

There really was a time before *Star Wars*. Anyone born in 1970 or afterwards might find that hard to imagine, but there was a time when audiences first watched those words rising from the bottom of the screen and slanting their way back into space, telling us that long, long ago there were heroes. There was a time before The Force.

Except for Stanley Kubrick's bold experiment of 1968, *2001: A Space Odyssey,* science-fiction, science-fantasy seemed more than a little below what movies should be about. *The War of the Worlds* (despite its origins with H. G. Wells), *This Island Earth, Destination Moon* were B-budget, supporting features in a double bill. Or else you watched *Star Trek* or *Lost in Space* on television. There was a move towards more prestigious films when Disney released *Twenty Thousand Leagues Under the Sea* (1954) in a spate of widescreen movies based on Jules Verne stories. But, they did not prepare us for what George Lucas was evolving in his imagination. From 1977 to 1983, Lucas produced what are now episodes 4, 5 and 6 in his epic: *Star Wars, The Empire Strikes Back* and *The Return of the Jedi*. It is a pity he has chosen to write and direct the more mundane episodes 1, 2 and 3 – he needs the skills of a director more adept than himself at screen storytelling.

One of the critics' bugbears about the first *Star Wars* movie was its dialogue, often roundly ridiculed as banal. And, if you are a critic, you may be right. But, again, if you are a critic, you should have the skills to recognise the conventions of the space epic genre that Lucas was using. *Star Wars* is light years away from Shakespeare. Rather, it has the dialogue one expects of a comic strip, words in a bubble with the arrow pointing to the mouth of the speaker. The words are basic, easy for anyone to understand. They are colloquial (which runs the danger of being dated). They are brief. And, often, they are smart and ironic. They can also be words of broad popular wisdom with an incantatory tone that brings solemnity to the comic strip adventures. 'May the Force be with you'. You can't beat Alec Guinness as Obi Ben Kenobi, the Jedi elder and mentor, the Sage of the galaxies whose word was lore and law (and had religious overtones as well). Then came Yoda and revelations about the identity of Darth Varder, something that the newer prequels have the advantage to capitalise on. However, thirty years on, despite so many other screen heroics, Luke Skywalker, Han Solo and Princess Leia, their robots and the Force are still forcibly with us.

In fact, this is popular mythical stuff. One must still add 'popular' because some older academics are not yet persuaded that *Star Wars* is the stuff of the great traditional myths – which are verbal and poetic, their preference. *Star Wars*, however, is visual before it is verbal and that is what so excited and affected the younger audiences in 1977, something that their elders, who wanted elegant verse and something worth listening to, underestimated. *Star Wars* could make reference to all kinds of myths in its images. In the Galaxies, there are empires, there are knights, there are princesses and there is chivalry. Good versus evil. The characters are and create legends. They go to exotic places beyond those visited by Marco Polo or by Gulliver. There are strange creatures in the tradition of the Sphinx and the Cyclops or Gorgon of Greek myths and of medieval gargoyles. Columbus had three small ships to venture to the unknown edges of the world. Han Solo flies high-powered space ships into the beyond. It is a technological world and benign robots act as guides (as well as offering humour and sentiment). In the Galaxies, there are forces of light and there is 'the dark side'. The power of evil in the *Star Wars* films is almost absolutely potent in the Emperor and Annikin chose to be Darth Varder. This transition was the greatest strength of Episode III, *The Revenge of the Sith*.

Psychologists who deal with dreams and symbols quickly realised that *Star Wars* took its place with classic adventures in the outer world as well as the inner world. Luke and Leia love each other, but discover that they are twins. Luke, trained by the Jedi mentor of his father, has to confront, with sword, albeit laser, the evil power and discover that it is his father and that Luke himself has the dark side within him. Acceptance of the dark side can bring it into the light and healing and, as Jung would say, individuation and wholeness are possible.

President Ronald Reagan was on to something when, in the mid-80s, he named the Strategic Defence Shield being developed by the United States, 'Star Wars'. But, he was not so strong on fostering the more psychologically healing aspects of George Lucas's vision. One needs to go to the celebrated writer, Joseph Campbell, to appreciate the power of the audio-visual mythology and psychology. When Bill Moyers interviewed Joseph Campbell for six hours on Public Television, where did they hold the discussions? On George Lucas's ranch.

New directions

With the popularity of *Star Wars*, an example of a movie which influences and alters reality rather than merely reflecting it, the question was, where to go from here? Where did the mythmaking screenwriters and directors want to go – and where did the Hollywood producers and the money people want to go? Two alternatives emerged.

The first direction was to follow the comic strip lead, to take the popular heroes of the comic books and bring them to life as contemporary heroes. It had been done before, but not very successfully. It was more the domain of the old Saturday matinee cliff-hanging serials, *Flash Gordon* and *Ming the Merciless* or *Dick Tracy*. The movie breakthrough for this trend in heroes was Richard Donner's *Superman* (1978) with Christopher Reeve as Superman, alias Clark Kent. There were to be three sequels during the 1980s.

The second direction was to take a kind of comic strip hero, but someone who did not rely on unearthly powers or Jules Verne-like anticipated technology. Chronologically, the first was the Australian, *Mad Max* (1979), with Mel Gibson as the policeman whose family was destroyed by bikies and who became an avenging angel on the highways. However, he made his international mark with *Mad Max 2*, re-titled for the United States, *The Road Warrior* (1981). This was a hero who relied on moral righteousness, moral and physical strength. The third film, *Mad Max Beyond Thunderdome*, was released in 1985 and a fourth is planned for 2006 or later.

The best known example of this second direction is, of course, Indiana Jones. With Harrison Ford as archaeologist and academic Indiana Jones, *Raiders of the Lost Ark* (1981) caught the popular imagination with its venturing into and opening up worlds of the past while relying on the action adventure spirit of such characters as H. Rider Haggard's Alain Quartermain from such stories as 'She' and 'King Solomon's Mines'. Steven Spielberg directed. George Lucas produced and there were two sequels in the 1980s. While there were plans for yet another sequel before Harrison Ford got too old for the role, this film never eventuated and its popularity and box-office success were appropriated by Stephen Sommers' *The Mummy* (1999) and *The Mummy*

Returns (2001), with Brendan Fraser genially leading the action.

There was no lack of heroes in the 1980s and 1990s and, indeed, into the new century, though it needs to be pointed out that until now this has been mainly the preserve of men and more men, rather than women. Generally, the women have been subsidiary characters, there for decoration or romance. But gradually things are changing. In Stephen Sommers' movies, Rachel Weisz usually keeps pace with Brendan Fraser. There were two X-Men films but they were really X Men and Women. By the time of *Van Helsing* (2004), Kate Beckinsale as Anna Valerious is to all intents and purposes the equal of Van Helsing.

Popular heroes and pop heroes

Pop-heroes, like Mad Max, are heroes of instant folklore. Their creators take them seriously. They suggest that these characters are in the long tradition of mythical heroes from the times and lands of quests, endurance, ogres and witches, legends. They are like the popular heroes of mythical sagas that embody entertainment and dramatise the longings of people, their vision, their shadow images. And, since these are pop-heroes for now, their times and places are of the future, a world 'a few years from now' or the strange times towards which our nuclear, racist, materialistic world seems to be hurtling.

Max can find an honoured place in the company of popular heroes. While Max can't fly, that does not mean he can't look Superman in the eye. Max is a human superhero; he has no galactic powers, only his ingenuity; no high technological weapons, only his vehicles. Perhaps audiences find they are closer to Max than to the supermen.

The Max of the original film is a hero from futuristic science fiction. The setting is a short time from the present; society is decaying, Halls of Justice are ageing warehouse buildings, signs askew. While there are shops, country homes, railway stations and the suggestions of a lifestyle we are familiar with, reckless riders roam the roads on bikes, in cars, in packs. They speed, crash, terrorise, rape and kill. The police chase, do their duty as the power-controllers of the roads, show some humanity. Max's family is killed and, in the tradition of the apocalyptic avenging angel, he pursues the guilty to the death. In a society out of control, he is law and order. In a society of law and order chaos, his values prevail: justice to be restored by the avenging of the good, by the punishing of the evil.

This is where Max's behaviour can touch our sense of outrage at violent behaviour. It is not easy to observe calmly, let alone condone the wreaking of justice by the 'amoral vigilante'. But, in a society where the law is ineffectual and situations cry out for the righting of wrongs and appeals for justice and atonement for crime, the vigilante-figure embodies outrage. In a world of textbook virtue and sin, the armchair moralist would find such vengeance unacceptable. In an ugly, real world, solutions are not so easily come by. *Mad Max* shows the horror and grief – it does not say that we have yet become this society. We could.

The road-movie genre is blunt. Issues and characters are drawn broadly, directly, larger than life, in sweeping outlines. We are meant to respond accordingly. It is an ugly world. There is both good and evil. How can they be reconciled? Can they?

Mad Max 2 takes the hero a step further. Max is now presented as a mythical hero. The time setting is a more distant future, cleverly suggested by a newsreel collage highlighting energy crises, urban upheaval, nuclear warfare. In a violent world where small communities hoard precious petrol and bike gang scavengers besiege them, a narrator tells us that he remembers Max, the Road Warrior, tormented by the demons of his past, who defended the people with his strength and ingenuity and helped them escape through the desert to a new life. Max is photographed standing, at both beginning and end, an icon-like champion of the future. Once again, there is direct action, few words but spectacular stunts galore.

Difficulties arise in calling Max a hero. This is very much a matter of terminology. We generally know what we mean by hero, but with the study of legends, folklore and myths in recent decades, authors are trying to be more precise in their use of the term 'hero'. 'Hero' has a range of dictionary meanings ranging from the demi-god to the chief man in a story: man of super-human qualities, favoured by the gods, demi-god; illustrious warrior, one who has fought for his country, man admired for his achievements and noble qualities; chief man in poem, play or story. However, some would prefer to limit the word to signify a man who is in control of his fate and whose quest is of universal significance. This latter is certainly the hero of myth, the kind of hero that Max becomes in *Mad Max 2*.

It may be useful to consider some characteristics of folklore, legend and myth so that the status of Max as hero of myth can become clearer. Folklore is the preservation and study of traditional beliefs, especially in the form of sayings, advice, tales. Folkloric tales are enjoyable; they preserve memories or are memorials of celebrities, significant events that are of local interest. They may have a potential for wider appreciation, a more universal appeal, but this is not emphasised.

Legends are also traditional tales, but they glorify their heroes and heroines. Whatever the historical facts associated with the figures of legend, the embroidering of the stories is more important. The figures of legend are larger than life. They become models for inspiration. Once again, they are local but have a potential for universal appreciation. But this is not stressed.

The original *Mad Max* presents a local hero caught up in the lawlessness of his times, who combats violence and, by violence, copes with his own grief and outrage. The story of his skills and his exploits is the stuff of futuristic science-fiction folklore. To the extent that Max is the best of the police patrollers, with human qualities as well as being the destroyer of the callous enemies of society, his mighty deeds can be remembered, retold with verve and admiration so that Max can become a legend.

However, the Max of the sequel becomes a hero of futuristic myth. Myth was studied in the context of religion. This has been extended to what might be called 'secular myths' by analogy with religious myths. The religious myth has been defined as 'a sacred story of a primordial event that constitutes and inaugurates a reality and determines man's existential situation in the cosmos as a sacred world.' It therefore deals with what are called 'limit-situations': birth, initiation, death.

Unfortunately, many still consider myth as something 'false'. Yet, the meaning of myth is in the truth told about the human condition, which is quite different from historical veracity or accuracy of reporting. There is a depth in mythic truth that cannot be communicated solely by accurate presentation of facts or truthful communication of information.

Myth, then, is a form of story that really creates a world of meaning. The stories will have local origins and be presented with local references, but they will have a universal appeal. Audiences of widely different cultures and experiences will still be able to respond to their insights and link them with their own myths. Because of the complexity of our human condition and experiences, there are many seeming contradictions, antagonistic contradictions that we have to contend with. Our myths have to help us grasp the paradoxical elements and strive to reconcile them in ourselves or in our society. We can think of such paradoxes as: beauty and order versus chaos, survival versus death, peace versus violence, justice versus vengeance, selflessness versus selfishness, heroism versus 'me first', courage versus fear.

The classical myths continue to have great appeal, even if contemporary audiences do not subscribe to their religious worldview – be it that of Greek tragedy or the Christian-pagan clash visualised in such 'Arthurian' films as *Excalibur*,

Dragonslayer, King Arthur. But for a diversely pluralistic and secularised society, the future rather than the past is the locale for myth. Science fiction has moved from the wonders of Jules Verne's fantasy, through Saturday matinee serial pulp entertainment to a new status, providing the imaginative landscapes, spacescapes, for the new clashes of values and the acting out of the highest and deepest human aspirations.

The most basic story in the myths is that of a journey. It is always a quest. This means that, on the way to the goal of the quest, there are tests, ordeals of endurance that uncover some of the weaknesses of the hero, but also challenge his strengths. Max now becomes the hero, a bitter 'me firster' in black clothes and vehicle, who uses his ingenuity, makes deals, but is also compassionate and courageous. Desperate needs challenge his generosity and he becomes a leader to salvation and promised lands.

The landscape of Max's world is an isolated desert community: the population is old and young, men and women, wise leaders, skilled mechanics – enough to portray a microcosm of the future. The enemy, by stark contrast, is a scavenger society, a vermin group of sub-humans – fiercely masculine, led by a mutant Humungus, a Mohawk-brute Wez with his Golden Boy cycle companion. A few women are glimpsed merely as sexual objects for the scavengers.

The past is evoked in costume and decor. The community is dressed in white with costumes influenced by medieval robes or classical styles. The scavengers are war lords, marauding warriors, with mock armour, Viking helmets. While Max is unsmilingly serious in black leather, the secondary hero, the Gyro Captain, looks like a humorous parody of a World War One ace, a Grubby Baron. While *Mad Max* ends as a grim, even despairing legend, *Mad Max 2* ends as a myth of rebirth.

This meant, of course, that expectations were high for *Mad Max Beyond Thunderdome* (1985) – that the third episode would improve on the previous two films. One of the aims was to develop Max as a character, to tell a 'more human story'. Mel Gibson remarked in interviews, 'In the *Road Warrior* Max was a sort of closet human being. In *Thunderdome* his protective layers are peeled away. There's a lot more depth, variety and humanity to the man.'

Max is still an obvious hero. The lyrics of the *Beyond Thunderdome* theme proclaim that 'we don't need another hero'. Out of the desert, this hero comes to right wrongs and lead lost children to safety and to rebuild, physically and spiritually, a new world. Max is hero enough.

The basic symbol of *Beyond Thunderdome*, as of the previous films, is the journey, both through the desert to a new promised land and Max's own interior journey from isolation to commitment. The journey, undertaken for others, becomes a spiritual quest. In the traditional myth, the hero is tested on the journey and his qualities of courage and endurance come to their peak. Again, in the traditional stories, the evil powers that attempt to control the destiny of the hero and put obstacles in his path tend to be symbolised by the witch and the ogre. In Bartertown, the ogre is a complex combination of gentle giant and intelligent dwarf. The witch, a beguiling one, is Tina Turner's Aunty Entity. The writers of *Beyond Thunderdome* have ensured that the basic ingredients for myth are contained in their screenplay.

With their pop culture style, the films are more like animated comic strips, strong, sharp and clear delineation of characters and situations, straightforward plot lines, larger-than-life treatment, funny, melodramatic, and occasionally slam-bang. It reminds us how the comic-strip style is a valid and effective twentieth century mode for myth-making, where strength and persuasiveness lie in their psychological credibility, despite the heightened characters and events.

This brings us to the meaning of the myth of *Beyond Thunderdome*: the post-nuclear world, the future society, the saviour-figure and the vision.

The post-nuclear world. While the film opens with striking helicopter shots of desert, the audience is plunged into the radio-active relic village, Bartertown, a grimy, dark-alleyed collection of buildings, a market centre reminiscent of feudal times, whose wares are more often broken modern technology. This ugly world has an underworld, a steaming grand sty where pigs grovel and guzzle and excrete to provide the power for Bartertown to survive. High above the people is the ruler's domain, a variation on a tree cubby-house but where law and power are taken as serious games. The central focus of Bartertown is Thunderdome, a geodesic dome building, an indoor coliseum where gladiators swing and fly in to-the-death combat. Bartertown says that our future-world is poisoned, struggling for some order, surviving but barbarous.

By contrast, across the sand-blown desert and away from the wreckage of a jet, is the oasis called 'The Crack in the Earth', caves, a pool, greenery, an Eden of lost children who live in hope. Finally, in a grim realisation for local audiences, there is Sydney itself, recognisable in outline, a broken bridge and the dust and darkness of a nuclear night, a sad promised land where children sit among the ruins attempting to learn about the past and begin rebuilding. Before they find their home, Max and the children must go back out into the desert for a final struggle to elude the machines.

This is the world of the future. What of future society? The population is small, isolated, cut off by disaster from its roots and similar communities, forced back on survival values and dog-eat-dog tactics of power-hunger and greed. Jedediah, the comic Bruce Spence, immediately swoops out of the sky and steals Max's camels and exchanges them in Bartertown. Bartertown's inhabitants look filthy, furtive, avaricious, either slinking around, aggressively double-dealing but coming alive like the bread and circus audiences of Roman empire gladiatorial combats at Thunderdome. They are stimulated by blood-lust. The hierarchy symbolise this society, from Frank Thring's obscenely bored, eye-patched Collector to Angry Anderson's punk-angry guard and Aunty Entity, Tina Turner embodying energy, chain-mailed, grasping her bow, strutting in her loft, swinging down into Thunderdome, making seductive deals with Max, upholding her law and order philosophy and exuberantly enjoying the battles. Society is cruel, eerie, corrupt.

In the bowels of Bartertown are the slaves, chained and condemned to work among the pigs. Ironically, one of these, the Pig Killer, is one of the cheeriest individuals, helping Max to escape and sending a dog carrying a water-can out into the desert to sustain him. But in this underground is the power to confront Aunty Entity and her attempts to impose law and civilisation: the Master-Blaster stoker, powerful in brain and brawn, yet a composite of giant with crippled dwarf. In the deadly battle in Thunderdome, introduced by the satanic-smiling compere, Dealgood ('Dyin' time's here') the brawn is paradoxically revealed to be a gentle giant, a baby-faced man whose innocence was controlled by the powerful mind of the dwarf.

The inferno is peopled with distorted creations parallel to those of renaissance painters with the hell of last judgements, human gargoyles that suggest mythical monsters that, in fact, are guttering and spouts. The human beings are part of a literally radioactive civilisation; they are plagued and plague-ridden.

The contrast is, as so often in myths, with the desert. The desert is a place of survival but also of purification, self-discovery. While pilot Jedediah and his son have a trap door from sand to haven of hoarded loot (which they can and do sacrifice for others), the desert is refreshed by oases, cracks in the earth, pools and waterfalls, cool caves and verdant slopes.

Here the society is in direct contrast to that of Bartertown – children, their memories clutching to images of skyscrapers and a technological past that has betrayed them. The hulk of their jet is set like a whale stranded on wind-blown dunes. They are suspicious of adults but, like older wanderers of the Australian desert, paint their aspirations on cave walls and yearn for a saviour. They recite and gesture their oral history, childlike and sing-song, and hope that the stranger, Max, is the one that they had hoped and longed for. This 'tribe' of children, boys and girls, hunters and guides, mothers, becomes, by default and by yearning, a chosen people (some with doubts who are swallowed up by the desert, some wise fools, others trusting disciples).

In their search for home they, like Max, are pitted against Bartertown-on-wheels led by the laughingly vindictive warrior queen, Entity, and her frequently destroyed but indestructible henchman. Out in the desert, after the nuclear Armageddon, the forces of light, pursued by the forces of darkness, clash with their enemies and win. The gloom of Bartertown gives way to the hope of the children. In the ruins of Sydney, they begin again, passing down their tradition, so that the resilient human spirit can live and create anew. 'We don't need another hero'; all we need is to go Beyond Thunderdome. What began in pessimism is transformed into optimism. The audience is invited to participate in a journey from despair to hope. *Beyond Thunderdome* is set in an aftermath of the end of the world. But it is not the end of the world.

Comic book heroes and masks

Although Superman was introduced to the post-*Star Wars* audience in 1978 in the guise of Christopher Reeve, and there were three sequels (and *Supergirl*), interest in the wider range of comic book heroes did not develop until the late 1980s. This came with the surprising success of Batman embodied by Michael Keaton. Part of the fun of the Superman films was the over-the-top performance of Gene Hackman as the arch-villain, Lex Luthor. The big star villain became a feature of the Batman movies, led by Jack Nicholson as The Joker. The sequels had multiple star baddies, Danny de Vito (Penguin), Michelle Pfeiffer (Catwoman), Jim Carrey (The Riddler), Tommy Lee Jones (Two-Face), Arnold Schwarzenegger (Mr Freeze), Uma Thurman (Poison Ivy). Then came *Darkman, Daredevil, The X Men, Catwoman* as well as numerous parodies.

The most successful of all was *Spiderman* (with *Spiderman 2* being even more successful than the original).

Peter Parker must be one of the least prepossessing of comic book and screen heroes. He makes Clark Kent look like an extrovert. Gauche, shy, academic – a nice, quiet young man – he is transformed into a fearless saviour of victims of urban crime. Of course, it was not his own doing. He was accidentally bitten by a spider undergoing biological experiments and acquires such arachnid abilities as creeping up walls and spinning a super-strong web from his hands. He is not always able to save the day, especially in not being able to prevent his beloved guardian, Uncle Ben, from being shot. Nor can he reveal his true emotions to the girl next door, Mary Jane, whom he loves. His awkwardness, however, does give him sufficient cover for people never to dream that he might be Spiderman. He must also combat cosmically destructive villains, Willem Dafoe as the Green Goblin and, even better, Aldred Molina as Dr Ock.

What is surprising in *Spiderman 2* is that we see far more humanity and complexity in a comic book hero than before. We have been prepared for it by Bruce Wayne's quiet moroseness and anguish about his parents in the Batman series, by Wolverine's search for his origins in the *X Men* films and the blinded Matt Murdock as *Daredevil*. But Tobey Maguire's Peter Parker is as complex as characters he has played in such serious films as *The Ice Storm* or *The Cider House Rules*.

It's all to do with masks

If we want the pop treatment masks and how masks can cover the real self but can manifest all kinds of wild desires from the sub-conscious and the unconscious, we need only to watch again *The Mask*, Jim Carrey's tour-de-force as the little man who is transformed into a mix of monster and clown by putting on a mask. But on a more intellectual note, one of the pleasures of watching *Kill Bill 2* (though 'pleasure' does not seem quite the right word for responding to *Kill Bill*, especially the overwhelming body count of Volume 1) is listening to a speech made by Bill to try to explain to Bridget why he has acted as he has. We were all eager to hear this because his excessively violent reaction to her leaving him provoked a bridal rehearsal massacre and a consequent rage rampage to end all rampages.

Instead, Quentin Tarantino gives David Carradine, as Bill, a fascinating address on the nature of comic book heroes and their use of masks. He explains how, for most heroes, their extravagant costume is the mask: Batman, Catwoman, Daredevil.... However, Bill makes a fascinating psychological point. He reminds us that it is quite different for Superman. Superman was born a super-hero on the planet Krypton. We saw the sequences of his coming to earth from outer space, that he had been endowed with the fullness of knowledge by his father, Jor-El. The hero needed a disguise when he came to earth. He needed a mask. The mask is really the bespectacled, self-consciously clumsy, Clark Kent.

Quentin Tarantino (like Kevin Smith in *Star Wars*) can write pretty smart post-modern dialogue on anything from Burgers Royale in Amsterdam (*Pulp Fiction*) to dissecting Madonna's image (*Reservoir Dogs*) or an elaborately gay reading of *Top Gun*. This speech on masks sounded very good and thoughtful – until *The Observer*'s critic, Philip French, remarked that the speech came from the introduction to a 1960s book on *Great Comic Heroes* by cartoonist and author, Jules Ffeiffer. Tarantino didn't have a footnote in *Kill Bill* referring to his sources. That seems to be a post-modern thing to do. But, coming from Ffeiffer through Tarantino, it was still a pretty good piece of discourse.

In the realm of masks and comic book heroes, Spiderman stands out. His fairly elaborate costume, red and blue with Perspex eyes, completely disguises Peter Parker – though he does complain to a young woman travelling with him in an elevator that it tends to cling, climb and clutch. When, in the first film, Peter is accidentally bitten by the spider, the result is that his heroic shadow side is liberated. It becomes his 'face to the world', but it also keeps his inner self secret.

In *Spiderman 2*, there is quite a psychological development and revelation. Director Sam Raimi is no slouch at comic book films. Apart from his *Evil Dead* movies, he directed the intriguing *Darkman* where Liam Neeson portrays a scientist whose face is burned and scarred in an experiment gone wrong and who dons mask, hat and cloak à la Phantom as he goes about wreaking revenge and pursuing justice. Raimi deserves our congratulations for having made the *Spiderman* films, original blockbuster movies that blend comic-book fantasy derring-do with humane sensibility and humour.

Spiderman 2 is an assured film, the makers confident in their abilities to provide exciting and entertaining action, along with some spectacular stunt work (crashing and rolling cars, chases up the sides of walls, a fight on top of a speeding train), with computer graphics to create a New York which is really a US Metropolis, and a tour-de-force villain, complete with vicious mechanical octopus-like appendages. But, Raimi has no hesitation in quietening the action to spend a lot of time exploring the intense and complex personality of Peter Parker.

This time Peter is still the shy, even clumsy introvert. Now he is unable to hold down a pizza-delivery job, he is failing in his studies, inarticulate in his inability to express his love for Mary Jane, awkward in relating to his Aunt May, blaming himself for selfishly being the occasion for his Uncle Ben's being shot, unwilling to tell his friend, Harry, the real identity of Spiderman since Harry vows revenge on Spiderman as responsible for the death of his father.

His work in keeping law and order and rescuing those in danger means that Peter has difficulty with his true identity. His inner potential, a more extraverted hero, emerges when he is Spiderman. He has a highly developed sense of responsibility and duty which he sees as requiring self-sacrifice in renouncing his love for Mary Jane, especially since Spiderman's enemies would put her life at risk (which they do). Aunt May gives him a strong pep talk about the need for heroes, pointing to their young neighbour, who wants

Spiderman to return since Peter feels that he has spoiled his life and has retired from his crusade.

As himself, Peter Parker could easily pass for one of those types whom the get-up-and-go doers cannot fathom: intense, tenacious, awkward, absent-minded, indecisive. He cannot find any way in which to communicate his deep love to Mary Jane. One of the most telling features of *Spiderman 2* is that, at one stage, he rushes into a burning building to rescue a child, but he does so as himself, Peter, not as Spiderman. His extroverted mask behaviour has taught him some self-knowledge and acceptance.

But what is really surprising, and a sign of his growing maturity as Peter is that several times and in key scenes, he takes off his mask and reveals his identity. The people in the speeding train remark that the hero who has saved them 'is just a kid'. When he confronts Dr Ock and appeals to his conscience, he becomes Peter Parker rather than the Spiderman Ock has pledged himself to destroy. Ock is repentant and redeems himself in his death. Peter is courageous enough to reveal himself to Harry and, by telling the truth, to run the risk of losing his best friend. And he finally reveals himself and his love to Mary Jane, who is only momentarily surprised and supports him in his saving the city. He does not depend or rely on the mask or the costume to be authentic.

Obviously, the Peter Parker of the two *Spiderman* films is not just a one-dimensional hero. He is a complex character, reflective and growing. This development means that the comic book heroes are not only responding to the need in the audience for another hero. It means that Spiderman is answering many questions about maturity and responsibility.

At the time of its release in 2002, many leaders, including church officials, gave interviews on the importance of having role models like Peter Parker/Spiderman in today's troubled atmosphere. Such a reference to the potential religious dimensions of these heroes is not new. Soon after the release of *Star Wars* and *Superman*, American commentator, Robert L. Short, who had written some insightful small books on the religious implications of the Peanuts' cartoons, published a book of his lectures on the space and heroes movies. He called it *The Gospel from Outer Space*. He highlighted some of the parallels of the space movies to the Gospels. In commenting on Luke Skywalker, he referred to 'The Gospel according to Luc...as'. He elaborated the themes of ET, which Steven Spielberg had intended as a 'Peter Pan from outer space' fable. Writer Melissa Matheson had a Catholic education and, while she wrote ET to Spielberg's instructions, she went to the studio one day, 'and then I noticed the Christ resemblances'. ET's final instructions to Elliot and the children are a variation on the end of Matthew's Gospel. The children are promised that ET will always be with them and they are to be good.

This kind of religious connection was immediately seen in *Star Wars* with the paralleling of The Force with the Holy Spirit in the cosmic struggle between good and evil.

One of the most interesting specifically religious links with the heroes comes in the opening forty minutes or so of *Superman: the Movie*. This section was written by Mario Puzo, author of *The Godfather*. It is serious stuff full of biblical and theological references. After that, the film seems to make a 180-degree turn and go back to the broad strokes of comic action and comedy. But, in Puzo's scenario, parallels are made between the little Krypton child and Jesus. Just as Jesus (in rather over-literal imagination) is said to come to earth from 'up there', so does Superman (and so does ET). Our glimpses of 'up there' are of a planet on the brink of explosion and extinction. As the baby's parent prepare to send him to earth to safety, the father is given dialogue straight out of St John's Gospel where Jesus speaks about his unity with the Father, how the Father lives in the Son and the Son in the Father. Whoever sees the Son sees the Father. This is what Jor-El (Marlon Brando having an opportunity to play God the Father after being The Godfather) says to his son. He then sends him to earth in a spacecraft that is designed as part crib and part star, like the one shining over Bethlehem. There used to be a theological hypothesis that all knowledge had been 'infused' into the mind of the human Jesus. In *Superman: the Movie*, as the child hurtles towards earth and begins to grow in age and wisdom, the father's voice is heard in a continual 'infusion' of all knowledge and history of earth. No wonder, Superman will need a human mask to conceal his prodigious knowledge and power.

In the movie, when the craft hits earth, Mr and Mrs Kent from Smallville, middle America, happen to be driving past. Bewildered (like Mary and Joseph in the Gospels), they see the child work a miracle in lifting the vehicle that is pinning down Mr Kent. They adopt the child, becoming his foster parents and take him back to their home where he remains until he is about thirty and begins his public life. How many people in the audience noticed these connections is anyone's guess. However, they are there and have the power to enrich enjoyment of the heroic action.

The Matrix

Film-makers are still drawing on the world's religious traditions and mythologies to give their films status. The most successful franchise in achieving this belongs to the Wachowski Brothers, Andy and Larry, and their *Matrix* trilogy. With the release of *Matrix Revolutions* in 2003 and the enthusiastic response to the religious references in all three films, a commentator on Vatican Radio spoke a too-well-publicised diatribe against the Hollywood pilfering of Christian symbols. The commentator would have done better to applaud the Wachowskis for actually including these symbols and for providing an opportunity for audiences to enjoy more serious discussion about meaning and religion. (Commentators had no difficulties in following through with the Christian parallels in *The Lord of the Rings* trilogy.)

With *Matrix Revolutions*, the Wachowski Brothers completed what has been one of the most popular and talked about film trilogies. While *The Lord of the Rings* dramatised

Tolkien's world and took its audiences into the mythical past and used religious symbols and motifs, *The Matrix* trilogy takes audiences into a future that is no less mythical and which also uses religious symbols and motifs.

When *The Matrix* (1999) was released, audiences both young and old responded to its exploration of the relationship between humans and modern technology. Philosophers around the world hurried to write articles for academic journals on how it raised the problems of what is real, what exists only in the mind and the possibilities of co-existing dimensions. Noted Catholic Polish director, Kzrystoff Zannussi, a member of the Vatican's Council for Culture was of the opinion that the film was a contemporary masterpiece and that people should see it, not only because of its extraordinary special effects but also because of its intellectual stimulus.

Matrix Revolutions, first screened around the world on the same day and at exactly the same time, no matter the time zone, followed *Matrix Reloaded* released six months earlier in 2003. Critics were not very enthusiastic about *Matrix Revolutions*. On the other hand, it became a talking point for religious educators and theologians. A world where human-created computers and machines now hold the humans to ransom and who burrow through the earth to destroy them and their refuge city, Sion, can only be saved by Neo, an anagram of the One.

The first film in *The Matrix* trilogy introduced Neo as a Saviour-figure, someone human (or programmed like one) to be the means of saving the human race. In death and resurrection imagery, he was killed and then loved back to life by the warrior, Trinity. In *Matrix Reloaded*, the saviour role of Neo is developed but left in abeyance. By *Matrix Revolutions*, Neo is still the Saviour-figure *par excellence*, referred to by his enemy, Bane, as 'the blind messiah'. In apocalyptic imagery, with overtones of biblical battle imagery, he saves the bereft humans in the city of Sion and confronts the Satan-figure, Mr Smith, and is seen, arms outstretched as on a cross. His blinded eyes see an internal vision, glowing beauty, a kind of 'beatific vision' that culminates in his final apotheosis.

While the Wachowski Brothers drew on all kinds of popular sagas and mythology, their use of names with Christian overtones for their characters, as well as imagery that is familiar from biblical stories, mean that there can be fruitful dialogue between the movie and the scriptures.

The descent of Jesus into 'hell' or 'Hades' or 'to the dead' is an article of the Apostles' and Nicene Creeds. Speculation in the early decades of the Church are echoed in references in Matthew's Gospel, the letter to the Ephesians as well as the suggested readings from John and I Peter. The tradition suggests that, while Jesus died for all, his death led him first to be associated with those who had gone before and were waiting to rise to new life with him.

The Jewish scriptures are full of battle imagery where God conquers the enemies of Israel as they do battle with their foes. The tour-de-force battle scene in *Matrix Revolution*, where the machines finally bore down to the city of Sion to destroy the humans, is replete with spectacular war machines, desperate human weaponry to ward off the enemy and terrible destruction of the humans. It is useful to read chapters 38 and 39 of Ezekiel, the chapter of Armageddon so beloved by fundamentalist and rapture Christians. Gog of Magog has a plan to destroy Israel but is no match for the power of God. God's warnings are given through the prophet. Perhaps the Wachowskis know Ezekiel. However, the machines are like Gog, overwhelming forces for destruction. The warriors of Sion are like the harassed people of Israel. Like Ezekiel, there is an Oracle who prophesies and guides, especially to lead the hero, Neo. These biblical battles provide a context for Jesus' descent to the Dead.

The overview is given in 1 Peter 3:18-20: Jesus' mission at his death is to go to those who have remained faithful, even if they have sinned, and rescue them. The letter uses a parallel with God's patience for those who remained faithful at the time of the deluge (and goes further to parallel the deadly deluge with the saving waters of Baptism). Now, the dead can be 'baptised' and saved through Jesus' presence.

Since Neo is the saviour, he is pictured in *Matrix Revolutions* going down into his own 'hell'. He is betrayed by Bane, blinded by him. But his inner vision leads him to guide Trinity above the machines to a safe vision of clear and beautiful skies before he descends to do battle with Mr Smith. Part of his 'hell' is the sacrificial death of his beloved Trinity. As the power of megalomaniac Smith (Satanic in its delusions of grandeur) seems to conquer him, he goes into a grave before he regains the strength (with the images of Neo, arms outstretched) finally to defeat Smith.

In this connection, the sayings of Jesus in John 5:24-30 are evocative: the special hour coming, the dead hearing the voice of Jesus, those good people in the tombs rising to new life because of Jesus doing the will of the Father who sent him on his mission. As Smith asks in bewilderment during their battle, 'Why?'. Neo answers, 'Because I choose to'.

Of course, many viewers will look at *The Matrix* trilogy as exciting science fiction or futuristic fantasy. Some will respond, according to producer, Joel Silver, just on the visceral level. Others will respond to the mythic layers. A Christian response will explore those mythic levels and discover the links between the scriptures, Jesus of the Gospels and the religious symbols. For audiences who are not sure of their faith or their biblical knowledge, the films provide aspects of a new apologetics, a contemporary invitation to examine the credibility of the Christian tradition.

The more explicitly religious reflections on *Star Wars, Mad Max, ET, Superman the Movie, The Matrix Trilogy* and the *Spiderman* films offer a deeper 'Yes' answer to the question of whether we need another hero.

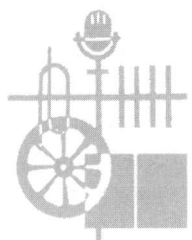

CHAPTER 4
Serendipity

Serendipity is a quality of happiness. It is part providence, part fate, part luck, part synchronicity or, as Bebe Neuwirth declares to Andie MacDowell and Gérard Depardieu in Peter Weir's *Green Card* (1990), after she has noticed a whole lot of detail that is French, 'It's what Jung calls... coincidence'. Whatever it means, it is a sweet-sounding word to begin a chapter that will look to the world of angels, even though it will have to deal with demons as well.

This chapter considers some aspects of how movie audiences perceive good and evil in the world. Strangely, even very strangely, adult people who reject traditional religion, especially Christianity, and who declare that they couldn't possibly believe in far-fetched and scientifically impossible doctrines about the incarnation of Jesus, the Virgin Birth, miracles... have no difficulty in talking in deadly earnest about Meg Ryan's death and Nicolas Cage giving up being an angel to be human in a romantic movie like *City of Angels* (1998) or a tongue-in-cheek, no-holds-barred bit of ecclesiastical demonology like *Stigmata* (1999), as if that is exactly how things are.

G.K. Chesterton is famously quoted as saying that when people stop believing in religion, it is not that they believe in nothing but that they believe anything. I was thinking about this issue in general while watching Denzel Washington as a Los Angeles detective in over his head in trying to deal with a demon who is able to move from person to person in *Fallen*

(1998). Towards the final climax, he asks a nun in a train whether 'Apocalypse' means anything to her and she replies in a pleasant common sense way, 'Revelation'. We then see him confronting and shooting the fallen angel Azazel, who had occupied the body of his police buddy, John Goodman (and who had a fairly foul mouth for contemporary swearing and cursing, but liked to sing 1960s songs like 'Time is on my side...'). He articulates an arcane text in (I think it was) Syro-Aramaic to keep Azazel alive so that Denzel could perform a ritual, running 600 cubits (or thereabouts) and make Azazel lose his breath (his spirit) and die. I wondered what Denzel was really thinking as he spoke those lines. Well, it was all acting, of course.

The movie finished and I pressed the stop button without glancing at what channel the television was on. I immediately heard someone anxiously declaring that the potion might not work and that he would have to return to his original demon state, or words to that effect. When I looked, there were these well-dressed modern twenty-somethings all talking about the occult, spells and demons as if they were everyday occurrences. It was only 7.30pm on a Saturday night. It was an episode of *Charmed*.

What on earth do people really believe about this world, the other world, heaven and hell? This chapter will take a look at popular movies that reflect on, fantasise about or create answers to these questions.

A Rumour of Angels

There was a great phrase going around in the 1960s, popularised by sociologist, Peter Berger, in his book about our capacities for being open to realities beyond what we can perceive through our five senses. He spoke of being alert to 'signals of transcendence' in our ordinary and extraordinary experiences. The title of his book and the significant phrase was *A Rumor of Angels: Modern Society and the Rediscovery of the Supernatural*.

Angels have had a chequered history. At the time that Peter Berger was writing, they tended to be dismissed as theological fairytales. They were mythical creatures that intervened in this world in the Biblical stories. They were the symbols who appeared in religious art, sometimes kneeling and adoring, sometimes as playful chubby cherubs with a penchant for lutes and lyres or ethereal nineteenth century asexual beings draped in formless nightie-like vesture. Not too difficult to relegate these figures to the folktale rubbish bin, except for the fact that people really seem to like angels and want to feel that they are around. Judaism, Christianity and Islam have no difficulty in telling stories of very active angels, many of whom are shared by these religions. The pantheon of Hindu deities reminds us that other world religions have their equivalents of angels.

Prior to the 1960s and the 'honest to God', 'death of God' debates about whether God was still alive and how we understood God (and God's angels), the movies liked to dabble in angelology. The famous archangels, Gabriel, Michael and Raphael made their appearances in the biblical, instructional, short films at the beginning of the twentieth century. The angel turning Adam and Eve out of the garden of evil (with his fiery sword) was popular and many apocalyptic angels, warriors as well as heavenly choirs, were seen on screen. However, there has always been a tendency where angels are concerned to have them a bit more 'up close and personal'. Hence the devotion in many churches to 'Guardian Angels'. The pious art of the nineteenth century was fond of these kinds of angels, sometimes strong, more or less male-looking beings, who sheltered people on their way. In one picture very popular in Catholic homes of the time, the angel stooped over little children playing by water, ready to stop them falling in or ready to dive in and rescue them. This picture was symbolic of many attitudes of adults towards angels, a childlike devotion that never grew up. Many adults, who would claim to have none or very little belief in angels, probably still imagine them lurking lovingly in the background.

Angels on screen

Who are the angels that have found their place in the movies? What are these angels expected to do? During the 1940s, there were several angel movies including *Angel on My Shoulder, Here Comes Mr Jordan, The Bishop's Wife* and the archetypal angel movie of them all, Frank Capra's 1946 classic, *It's a Wonderful Life*. It should be noted that, at least in the United States, *It's a Wonderful Life* is the Christmas movie. It is also the movie that is often playing in the background when a screenplay asks for a film to be showing. The movie secured an important and settled place in the filmgoer's psyche. And so did Clarence, the angel who is trying to earn his wings.

Hollywood angels are figments of a benign imagination. They have little or no connection with any of the doctrines of Christianity, except that the Scriptures posit these beings who come down from some kind of 'heaven' and have an existence between God and human mortals. Actual links between screen angels and biblical angels are very tenuous. However, the public responds well to the word angel and likes to see them on the screen.

What is the attraction of *It's a Wonderful Life*? Firstly, the central character, George Bailey, played by James Stewart, is Mr Middle America. He is the twentieth-century Everyman that anyone from a western culture can identify with. He is a kind of secular saint. He is not perfect, but his faults are not really blameworthy. He believes in people. He wants to do good. His dream is to go off to foreign lands to build bridges, but he never gets to leave Bedford Falls. His vocation is to help his friends and neighbours, to stand up for their rights when the Depression hits and greedy and tyrannical bank owners want to shut the doors of the banks and saving loans companies. He is willing to make restitution for the bad management of his uncle. Finally, this good man and devoted father and husband begins to snap at his wife and children. He becomes depressed and, in despair, is ready to throw himself off the local bridge.

Enter Clarence. The moral of *It's a Wonderful Life* is that human nature is basically good, but that human beings can be sorely tried. People often make the desperate comment that God should intervene to save those in despair. It is too frequently assumed that God does not intervene – and the theological argument is put forward that God has graced us with free will and, respecting that, does not intervene directly to change the course of history. But, it could be added, God intervenes indirectly, through family and friends, through circumstances that can change the direction of despair. This is where the rumour of angels fits in. Angels have become one of the symbols of hope that God does intervene in our lives and helps change them for the better. After all, angels are a more personal embodiment of the transcendent than abstract logic about God or philosophical or theological presentations. It is often easier to acknowledge angels than God.

Poor old Clarence, as played by the gentle character actor, Henry Travers, is really a bit of an elderly fuddy-duddy. Capra has been intuitively smart in helping audiences to be comfortable with Clarence. George is the good man. Mary, his wife is a good woman (after all, she is played by Donna Reed). We can all identify with his plight. He needs saving. And there is Clarence, a second-class angel (who gazes up at twinkling stars as if we all knew that this is where heaven is), who earns his wings by bringing George back to life, restoring him to his family, to the admiration of the town and to a very merry Christmas.

But the way that Clarence works is central to the influence of the angel. Because *It's a Wonderful Life* has been generally sweetness and light up to this point, the makers felt the need for a bit of the dark side. So, Clarence asks of George the very reasonable, but telling, question: what would your world be like if you had not been part of it? He takes George on a tour of a surprisingly squalid Bedford Falls, full of dens of iniquity, peopled by fallen men and women, a touch of hell on earth. George has really saved all these people by his goodness (which means that George is the one with the angelic touch).

There is no need for despair. George learns to be satisfied with his actual life. He can be happy. This is something of what guardian angels are supposed to do.

A more suave and sophisticated angel appeared in *The Bishop's Wife* (1947) in which the angel Dudley advises Episcopal bishop Henry Brougham (in one of the relatively rare movies where the Episcopal Church received prominence), who is struggling to build a cathedral with money donated by a rather demanding widow. Dudley was Cary Grant and the bishop David Niven. The work was taking its toll on the bishop and he found himself neglecting his family – with Dudley seeming to take his place. That put the bishop's wife (Loretta Young) in something of a spot, with two holy men in the house. But everything ends up happily and holily.

Another well-known angel of the 1940s was Mr Jordan, something of an accountant and emissary from God whose task in *Here Comes Mr Jordan* (1942) was to give a person who died accidentally – and whose soul an inexperienced angel had collected before time – a chance to redeem himself by taking the identity of a person who had finally died. Angels were thus entering into the personal judgment process and engineering a kind of spiritual reincarnation. Robert Montgomery was a boxer who died in a plane crash who has the chance to redeem the rather nasty personality of the murdered tycoon whose body he has assumed. One can see from this why angels had to earn their wings, especially if there were a number of over-eager and careless angels snatching souls prematurely!

That was the 1940s. There were some angels around in the 1950s, either comic helpers like Clifton Web and Edmund Gwenn in *For Heaven's Sake* and baseball aficionados who helped straggling players in *Angels in the Outfields*. Then angels went through something of a dark period in the 1960s and 1970s. There were, as we will see, more demons than angels. With the sceptical 1960s and such movements as 'the death of God', God's death tended to mean the death of angels with devils resurrected.

A substitute for angels in the 1970s was the more benign alien, the alien who did not abduct humans and subject them to all kinds of experiments, many (as some witnesses declare) of a proctological nature. The principal example of this genre was Steven Spielberg's *Close Encounters of the Third Kind* (1977). In fact, the aliens had a kind of angelic drawing power as well as a power of transformation for good akin to the activity of angels. At the same time Nicolas Roeg had David Bowie as *The Man Who Fell to Earth* (1976). Spielberg returned to this theme with *ET* (1982), who acts as a guardian angel to Eliot and his family, and Jeff Bridges was a friendly *Starman* (1984).

Yet, there has always been a yen for angels. A good source for checking this out is to listen to talk shows where listeners will phone in with some (rather incredible) stories of sensing angelic presence, experiencing angelic help and even apparitions. With the popular television series, *Highway to Heaven* and *Touched by an Angel*, angels gained media popularity and respectability.

Touched by angels

One of the reasons for considering *It's a Wonderful Life*, *The Bishop's Wife* and *Here Comes Mr Jordan* is that those very popular stories of angels in the 1940s transcended their original decade and were remade. The earliest of these and the most significant because it was released in the unlikely angel year of 1978 was the remake of *Here Comes Mr Jordan*. However, the remake took the title of another 1940s comedy that dealt with personal judgment and the devil having a hand in who went to heaven and who went to hell, *Heaven Can Wait*. Warren Beatty chose to direct and to star in this heavenly fantasy. It was popular at the time. Beatty played a baseballer. James Mason was a charming and dapper Mr Jordan. It was something of a shock to see this kind of angelic fantasy on the screen when the US was finally acknowledging the impact of the war in Vietnam in such films and Oscar winners as *Coming Home, The Deer Hunter* and *Apocalypse Now*. *Heaven Can Wait* reminded audiences that they were not really averse to some 'rumours of angels'.

There was a remake for television of *It's a Wonderful Life* called *It Happened One Christmas* (1977). It follows the original fairly closely except that, for the times, there was role reversal in the characters. Producer Marlo Thomas had the screenplay adapted so that Mary Bailey, played by herself, could go through the despair – which meant that Clarence became a female angel (Chloris Leachman). This reversing of roles thirty years after the original film is an indicator that, at least on screen, until then most of the angels were distinctly masculine.

The same is true of more recent years when the three angel films of the 1940s were remade for a new generation. But this time, they did not come alone. What is it about the latter half of the 1990s that angels became very, very popular? Some say that it is just another fad in New Age spiritualities. The angels in this context are not particularly biblical but are symbols of the need for 'feel good' stories and the perennial hope that there are guardian angels taking care of us and, maybe, connecting us to God or something divine out there. Some take a more serious tone and are happy that audiences have rediscovered angels on screen and may discover them in their personal and spiritual lives.

But there is a prominent feature of the re-makes of the three classics: two of the angels are African Americans and in two of them, the heroes who need the help of the angels are African American. One is tempted to use the un-English but very American phrase, 'Go figure!'

The first to be made was the 1996 remake of *The Bishop's Wife*. It stays in the ecclesiastical realm, but has gone a touch downmarket in terms of the hierarchy. The film is called *The Preacher's Wife*. And she is Whitney Houston in one of her rare screen appearances. The preacher who has something of the same problems as the Bishop half a century earlier, except that the American cities and neighbourhoods have gone down market and Dudley has to get his hands dirty, despite appearing in a suit and overcoat that mark him out as an affluent and dapper dresser. God does not niggle about prices for his emissaries. And he looks particularly good because he is Denzel Washington.

The Preacher's Wife is full of sentiment (and, for many a hardened viewer, sentimental). The difficulties of the preacher, the feelings of neglect by his wife, the abundant do-gooding of Dudley which ingratiates him with the preacher's family and with all the parishioners, mean that there is a whole lot of angelic good going on. *The Preacher's Wife* and the presence of Denzel Washington gave a fair amount of credibility to the possibilities of kindly angels amongst us.

Don Cheadle is of smaller build than Denzel Washington, short, skinny and cheeky, streetsmart. He is like a modern Dickensian Ghost that Might Have Been. The film is *The Family Man.* Cheadle does not have an immediate commanding presence, especially since he hangs around bars, and other unlikely places and does a hold-up in a convenience store. These are the kinds of places where a 1999 kind of Clarence ought to be to search out a contemporary George Bailey. And contemporary George Baileys are no saints. They promise the world to those they love and then fly off into the sunset, to a foreign land, to a successful, lucrative and powerful career where pledges and loved ones are consigned to oblivion. When our modern George (Nicholas Cage with the Everyman name, Jack) cannot get a taxi in New York City on Christmas Eve, it might seem like the end of the world to him. But he does a kind deed and his angel gives him the chance to see what his life might have been like – with a wife, a family and a demanding father-in-law who has trapped him in a tyre sales job that he hates. He even visits his company to see how it has developed without his skills.

Jack learns to appreciate having a family. He helps out the company with his knowledge and experience. He has the chance to meet his girlfriend again and resume his life with a stronger values base.

Perhaps that is what modern angels are supposed to do. They jog consciences, help their charges to re-examine their lives and re-shape them, reconstruct them on a base of integrity. A very much more serious angel guiding a lost man through life was Will Smith being the golf coach of Matt Damon in Robert Redford's *The Legend of Bagger Vance* (2001). With a slightly lighter touch, Delroy Lindo and Holly Hunter guided the lives of Ewan McGregor and Cameron Diaz in *A Life Less Ordinary* (1997) and Brad Pitt was a benign Death come to earth like an angel to find out what human life was like before he accompanied wealthy businessman, Anthony Hopkins, to the other side in *Meet Joe Black* (1998), itself a remake of a 1940s fantasy, *Death Takes a Holiday*.

And, yes, there was another re-make of Mr Jordan/Heaven Can Wait. It was specifically designed for the stand-up talents of African American comic, Chris Rock. He plays not a sports figure, but an aspiring comic who has a talent for deadening instead of deadpan. His version is called *Down to Earth* (2001). It is louder, more hip-hop with touches of the brash and the crass. The emphasis is on comedy with Rock springing good on unsuspecting cases, learning to overcome his selfishness and experiencing a little redemption. In keeping with the comic tone, Mr Jordan does not walk in the serious shoes of Claude Rains and James Mason. This time he is the ever-bumbling, double-take one-liner expert from *American Pie, Best in Show* and *A Mighty Wind*, Eugene Levy who is simply called Keyes. The film was adapted and directed by Chris and Paul Weitz who made *American Pie*.

Down to Earth, playing especially to African American audiences, and *The Preacher's Wife* and *The Family Man* indicate a continued desire for angels but acknowledge that this is a far tougher world that that of the middle of the twentieth century, that movies must show more than just something of the ugly world so that the good and honourable world will seem desirable. In fact, these re-makes tend to be sermons against self-centredness, dishonesty, greed and exploitation.

The fact that they are offbeat with touches of black comedy reminds us that we live in a world which continually needs the sharp comment of satire, that leaders need to respond to instant accountability in a worldwide linked society, that hypocrisy is prevalent but not believed in. With the certainties having less power to ensure personal, communal or societal security, humour is a way of coping with post-modern relativism. Which means that the screen has presented us in recent times with some pretty unusual and strange angels. Before we move on to the demons, they are worth some moments of consideration.

Angels' Wings of Desire

The name Wim Wenders needs to be mentioned. His breakthrough fantasy of 1987, *Wings of Desire*, in some critics' eyes is the angel film *par excellence*. One of the reasons for this accolade is that it is a German film, a European film and not a Hollywood film. It is serious angelology. Theologians from North-western Europe have held seminars on it, published many academic articles and books on it, taken very seriously these Berlin rumours of angels. It very much appeals to the sensibility of this part of the world. On the other hand, it rather tries the patience of more 'get up and go' audiences who acknowledge the value of the themes, but find themselves frequently shuffling in their seats.

The sequel, *Far Away So Close* (1993) takes up the same themes and some of the same characters in post-reunification Berlin (with Mikhail Gorbachev appearing as himself) and is a little more accessible to a wider audience.

Wenders was brought up as a Catholic but converted to Lutheranism, so he has strong theological foundations and insights for his story of angels who roam Berlin, looking down on the inhabitants from rooftops and from the statue of the Angel in the Tiergarten. They intervene to assist people in distress, listening in to their inner thoughts. One angel, Damiel (Bruno Ganz), fascinated by human life and attracted by a circus acrobat, decides to forfeit his angelic life and privileges and falls to earth to become human. Wenders seems to be saying that a spiritual existence, no matter how devoted and self-giving, is not enough. Human existence with the richness of its mortality, pain, joys and pleasures is a much fuller and fulfilling life. When one reflects on this theme – and many did with Wenders' films and with the Hollywood remake, *City of Angels* (1998) – the link to God becomes very clear. One might say that God did not find the divine life absolutely fulfilling but, out of love for humans, out of love for mortals, also fell to earth and became human. *Wings of Desire* is a plausible argument for the Incarnation.

Ten years later, Hollywood remade *Wings of Desire* as *City of Angels*, its setting – where else? – Los Angeles. *City of Angels* kept the basic plotline of the original as well as the theme of angels wanting to give up their protective mission and become human. Berlin had the advantage of historical buildings and monuments for the angles to perch on as they watched over the city. Los Angeles has skyscrapers and billboards! Berlin seemed more than a little chill with much of Wenders' black and white photography. *City of Angels* is bathed in a sunset glow. Nicolas Cage has never been more earnest. Meg Ryan is not a circus acrobat, but a heart surgeon. Guardian angels have their upmarket clients.

What is distinctive about *City of Angels* and creates a puzzle is that once the angel has fallen to earth, discovered other angels who have chosen to become human and is about to find earthly bliss with the woman he has so intensely guarded (even stalked!), she is suddenly and peremptorily killed, riding her bicycle, and the angel is left stranded on earth, alone and robbed of his destiny. Is this some Hollywood version of an *amour fou* ending in tragedy? Is the angel being punished for having departed the heavenly realm? Here was a story that needed a happy-ever-after ending. The angel was left with a complete self-sacrificing love.

Angels down and dirty

This downbeat tone pervaded another angel film of the period, *Michael* (1997) with John Travolta as the archangel himself. This time we have a down and dirty archangel, an angel as something of 'a regular guy', a kind of 'counter-angel'. Michael does angelic protective deeds, but he is not everybody's idea of an angel. When he appears, in fact, he looks like a slob, slovenly, shabby overcoat, pot-bellied, smoking, swearing and drinking, dancing à la Travolta and not above some flirting and sexual misbehaviour. Maybe the angel movies set the standard too high, that Denzel Washington's exemplary decency was a bit too highfalutin' for mere mortals who needed an angel that they could relate to.

Michael's mission is not one of the most noble ever ordained. He has to protect William Hurt as a cynical journalist working for a sensationalist tabloid much like *The National Enquirer*. He has to connect him with Dorothy (Andie MacDowell) for a happy ending. He does, and with the help of Jean Stapleton as an eccentric old lady who believes in angels and eventually becomes one to aid Michael in his mission.

Once again we have a kind of post-modern comic presentation of angels. In the past, they were heavenly, even ethereal. While crystals may be revelatory for New Age devotees, most people's very mundane lives seem to ask for more literal down-to-earth help, someone to share their experiences, both good and bad, who knows from the inside what human weakness is really like. Repentance and forgiveness are not a quick confession and absolution, but a reassessment of life with a serious purpose of amendment. Despite the fact that he looks like a street person about to ask for a handout, Michael, without his traditional sword and shining armour, is likeable even though the film is a bit of fluff from an angel's wingtips.

The down and dirty angels did not end there. The

twentieth-century angel movies came to their climax with Kevin Smith's *Dogma*. His friends, Ben Affleck and Matt Damon, portray two angels, Bartleby and Loki, lost in Wisconsin. They have a touch of the malicious about them, one of them responsible for God's punishments in the Old Testament), but are desperate to get back to heaven. If they can enter the portals of a church in New Jersey where a millennial indulgence is available to believers, they might just do it. However, it appears that if they can exploit this loophole, then it will destroy all that God has done for the earth, proving that you can get round God.

Kevin Smith is one of those cult figure directors with a smart line in offbeat dialogue and a comically rabid imagination, especially let loose in *Dogma* on the biblical tradition, the Catholic Church and some of the Jewish apocryphal stories. He is not averse to making up his own apocryphal stories – like having Linda Fiorentino as a descendant of Mary and so related to Jesus and the late twentieth-century Messiah-figure who takes on the mission of stopping Bartleby and Loki. He has Alan Rickman as Metatron, a rather asexual heavenly being whose appearance, demeanour and dialogue mock the traditional movie angel. He also has Chris Rock suddenly landing from the sky on the tollway, the thirteenth apostle who was eliminated from the Gospels because he was black! Kevin Smith is a new generation Catholic, born in 1971 and not brought up in the old-style parochial school staffed with nuns who taught catechism. Smith has a rather loose theology underpinning a faith in God that he likes to affirm publicly (as he does in the credits of his *Jersey Girl* (2003)).

With the picaresque adventures of the angels in *Dogma*, their only too human faults and frailties and some growing malevolence as they find their chance to return to heaven slipping from them, Smith is playfully but seriously asking what people really believe while mocking the eccentricities and superstitions associated with belief. This look at angels on the screen indicates that audiences like an angel story, that helpful guardian angels are more desired than not – but it is anybody's guess what form such an angel will take.

Demons

Dogma is a useful transition movie for angels and demons. If Loke, Bartleby, Metatron and co. were strange theological inventions by Kevin Smith, what about his demons and the devil? Jason Lee appears as a cynical American con-man devil, ever ready with smooth and semi-plausible temptations. But the devil...

Perhaps a few words of history and art context are in order. Put simply and politely, from medieval times at least, the devil is associated with scatological imagery. Chaucer, for instance, has no trouble in talking about some clergy as the devil's faeces. There are images of the devil dropping excrement, reproduced, for example, by Pier Paolo Pasolini in his version of *The Canterbury Tales*. Martin Luther is another well-known example. Having stayed in the realm of the technical aspects of scatology, we have to move into the vernacular when considering *Dogma*. Smith's characters are not averse to the 'shit' expletive. However, Smith prefers, among his frequent and varied bodily function jokes, to use the word 'poop'. And there you have it. From the literal bowels of the earth, a demon appears, consisting solely of poop, a large, odorous (well, stinking!), faecal devil. It has been remarked by spiritual sages that one of the best ways of coping with the devil and bringing him down to size is to laugh at him. Kevin Smith declares his belief in God, but he mocks the devil as a real shit.

If there were popular images of angels in the movies, especially since the 1940s, what about devils? Generally, the devil was presented with a light touch: the large Laird Cregar judging souls in *Heaven Can Wait* (1943), a cunning and gleeful Walter Huston as Mr Scratch making bargains with down and out farmers and having to be argued out of collecting by Daniel Webster (Edward Arnold) in *The Devil and Daniel*

Webster (1941), suave Ray Milland meddling in corporate politics in *Alias Nick Beal* (1949) and ultra-suave Claude Rains allowing a criminal to come back to earth to wreak havoc and revenge (but unable to do so) in *An Angel on My Shoulder* (1946). These films were entertainments, sometimes done with a light touch, sometimes presented as moral fables.

However, there was one rather frightening image of the devil from 1940 and that courtesy of Walt Disney. His *Fantasia* was a collection of short animated films to accompany the performance of popular musical classics like pieces of The Nutcracker Suite or Beethoven's Pastoral Symphony. Also included was Mussorgsky's' Night on the Bare Mountain which took its visual representation of the judgment of the wicked and the condemnation of the damned from the Renaissance art tradition of hell. Towering over them was a large, sinister, black-cloaked figure of Satan himself.

1966

Damien Thorne was born in Rome on 6 June 1966. Not only 666, but 6/6/66 – the Devil's numbers according to some interpretations of the Book of Revelation. Of course, Damien Thorne did not exist – except in the movies. Born in *The Omen*, raised in *Damien: Omen 2* and coming to adulthood and power in *The Final Conflict: Omen 3* (then some less distinguished sequels), Damien Thorne is the devil incarnate.

The point is that 1966 was a pivotal year, particularly in the English-speaking world, for faith and loss of faith. It was at Easter, 1966, that *Time Magazine* produced its now-famous cover, black and red-rimmed asking the question, Is God Dead? The first half of the 1960s was a tumultuous time: Berlin Wall, Bay of Pigs, Cuban missiles, JFK assassinated, the Vietnam War, the extent of the drug culture, hippydom and free love… Theologians asked questions about the realities of God, so many wondered, is God dead?

Asking this question meant that another question could be

asked. If God is dead, is the Devil dead? For many, the obvious answer was 'yes'. But, just as a sense of the presence of God lurks in many people's semi-conscious, so does a sense of the presence of evil, the devil. What *Time Magazine* and others were not to know was that the Devil was about to have a cultural resurrection, in books and in the movies and in quite a spectacular and box-office success.

The first sign of the return of the devil came in 1968 with the release of Roman Polanski's *Rosemary's Baby*. In a coven in New York City a group of witches deceive a young woman, Rosemary (Mia Farrow), into becoming the mother of the incarnate Satan. If it was conceivable that the human could become divine, that Jesus was God in human form, then it was just as conceivable that Satan could also take human form. This was not the kind of doctrine reflected on in theological halls. However, Ira Levin's bestseller and Polanski's film caught the imagination and a new genre of devil films (some of them actually rather diabolical!) was unleashed. With the unserendipitous tragedy that befell Roman Polanski in August of that same year, the murder of his wife Sharon Tate and her friends by Charles Manson and his family, images of evil and hellish malevolence were in the air.

Five years later, Hollywood released another film on the devil's activity. There had been a long tradition, based on Gospel texts where Jesus cast out demons, that devils could enter and possess a human being, transforming them sometimes into blaspheming creatures and doing them physical and mental damage. The tradition continued and was often associated with reputable saints, that the devil could take hold of them and would not leave until special rituals were performed by ministers set aside for these specific purposes, exorcisms. *The Exorcist* was a big budget production which was nominated for several Academy awards and was based on a bestseller by William Peter Blatty, allegedly based on actual events which took place in Georgetown DC in the late 1940s.

The impact of *The Exorcist* in 1973 was enormous. Both

the movies of *Jesus Christ Superstar* and *Godspell* were released in that same year and were also successful. But *The Exorcist* grabbed the headlines and the ticket sales. The respected reviewer in *The New Yorker*, Pauline Kael, referred to it as the biggest pro-Catholic poster since *The Bells of St Mary's*. She saw it not as attacking the Catholic Church and its practices, but rather as giving credibility to doctrines and beliefs. While non-Christians saw the film as just another variation on horror movies, Christians found it believable. It was remarked at the time that the people who would fear it most would be lapsed Catholics who had been brought up with these beliefs, had rejected them but now saw them presented on screen with some plausibility.

What the film was saying to the audiences of 1973 was that, just as angels could guard and protect human beings, so devils could not only tempt humans to sin, but could actually enter into their bodies and minds and take possession of them. Angels never take possession of us. They care and protect. Devils, who are considered fallen angels, can destroy us from inside. With the death of God or, at least, God seeming distant and/or unreal to many people, Chesterton's dictum was seen to be truer than ever. Loss of faith in God meant believing in anything. If we look at the catalogue of films about the devil or about devils made since 1968, they are, to use a word the devils themselves used on the cliffs above the Sea of Galilee, 'Legion'.

The third of the prestigious devil films was *The Omen*. Some of the respectability by this stage was the presence of Gregory Peck as the father of the demonic child. Lee Remick was the mother. The screenplay drew on the specific religious aspects of the interpretation of the Book of Revelation, the rituals of exorcism and the destructive activity of the devil. Because *Rosemary's Baby* had brought diabolical incarnation into the popular mentality, audiences had no difficulties in accepting Damien as the devil in human form. This continued two years later with the first sequel, paralleling the Gospel stories with Damien living a hidden life before he emerged for his mission to the world in the second sequel in 1981. However, the screenplay made a contrast with the Gospel stories. Whereas Jesus lived a poor and hidden life in Nazareth before he began his mission of salvation, Damien grew up in an affluent American family with business and political connections, just the place for the devil to be.

When Damien finally emerges to gain control of the whole world, he is the Chief Executive of a multinational company and ambassador to Britain. The fervid imagination plot has Jesus being born again in England. Damien engineers the killing of all the children born at that time so that Jesus will be destroyed. Damien is a latterday Herod plotting against the Innocents. He is now truly and literally the Antichrist.

At the time of the release of *The Final Conflict*, and despite the 18-Restricted certificate, school girls all wanted to see the film because of Sam Neill. At this stage of his career, Sam was a handsome devil and the girls were finding the devil very attractive. They were even carrying heavy bibles to school to look up the quotation from Revelation that they had heard in the film. Here they were, quite prepared to leaf through the bible because of an image of the devil whereas they would not look at the bible because of Jesus. A case of believing anything – especially as the text was composed by the screenwriter for dramatic purposes. While the devil, according to the scriptures, can quote them for his own purposes, writers are inventing them for their own purposes – and getting a larger following of disciples.

One other feature of devil-films was introduced in the late 1970s. It raised the question of where did the demons come from and how did they get to earth. If the angels came from somewhere up there, then the devils must come from somewhere down there. Once again the screenwriters took up the imaginative challenge. They were intrigued by the phrase 'gates of hell', a phrase used in a number of religions.

Most of the gates of hell were to be found in the United States! A second location was Italy, which seems fair enough. The Italians, never to be outdone in exploitation movies, had known great success with several sword and sandal adventures based on Greek mythologies. When that passed, they made their own westerns, with even greater success. They were acknowledged as 'spaghetti westerns'. As the popularity of these films abated, they found a new spaghetti genre, the diabolical horror genre (once again relying on older American stars to give them some international status). There were such titles as *House of Exorcism* (with Telly Savalas), *The Antichrist* (with Arthur Kennedy), and *Holocaust 2000* (with Kirk Douglas).

While *The Sentinel* posited the gates of hell in an apartment block in New York City, the principal location for devil entry was in the New England town of Amityville (a touch of irony with such a peaceful name). The popularity of diabolical dealings in a seemingly possessed house in Amityville led to three sequels and discussion in 2004 about a remake. One of the effects of *The Amityville Horror*, which was advertised as being based on a true story, is that many (too many) in the audience accepted everything as fact. Where is Amityville, can you visit the house, can you see where the devil enters this world? There were probably more people prepared to make a pilgrimage to Amityville than to Loreto, in Italy, where the holy house of Nazareth is alleged to be.

Angel/Devil

The ambiguities concerning God and the devil, angels and demons, were also dramatised in movies, a theme that is of perennial interest. One of the traditions about the appearance of demons is that they do not necessarily have to breathe fire and brimstone, but rather can be more attractive in appearance than angels of light. This theme has stimulated film-makers and is much more spiritually challenging than the melodrama of possession. This is the theme of the mysterious stranger who may be good or may be evil. The stranger enters a home or a community and transforms everyone for better or worse.

On screen, one of the most arresting examples of this

genre was Pier Paolo Pasolini's *Teorema* (1969). Pasolini, a Marxist author and director, had made a strong impact, especially on cinema critics who decried the blandness and sentiment of the Hollywood Jesus films, with his 1964 stark, black and white *The Gospel According to St Matthew*. His *Teorema* was a film of temptation and challenge. Terence Stamp was a kind of angelic presence who appeared, took lodging with a family, and tested their values and stances, including their sexuality. Stamp was both saving angel and tempting devil. When *Teorema* was awarded the International Catholic Film Organisation's prize at the Venice Film Festival, the organisation was condemned by a number of church authorities, who considered the film offensive if not blasphemous. This was the atmosphere of the late 1960s. Those who had been overwhelmed by the changes of the decade, or who were resisting, for instance, the injunctions of the Second Vatican Council to be open to the 'signs of the times' and to engage with the world and contemporary questions and issues, preferred words of strong condemnation to dialogue.

Other examples of this genre on a more secular level were the film version of Joe Orton's *Entertaining Mr Sloane*, with Peter McEnery as the mysterious handsome stranger, and Hal Prince's *Something for Everyone* with Michael York as the stranger. Acclaimed English writer, Dennis Potter, wrote a similar story for television and then for cinema where the genial stranger who insinuates himself into an ordinary British home and, after charming the family, wreaks destruction is in fact, the devil. The title contained overtones of hell and suburbia, *Brimstone and Treacle*, with Sting as the stranger.

This kind of stranger also appears in several westerns directed by Clint Eastwood, where he plays the central roles. Already in his second film, *High Plains Drifter* (1972), Clint plays a rider who appears out of the haze and settles in a frontier town. At first, he seems to be a Christ-figure. He protects the widows and the orphans, getting them out of the town before he paints it red and puts up a sign near the lake beside which the town is built. The sign reads HELL. He then sets the town alight, at night, standing in the centre, cracking a whip on the 'sinners', a kind of avenging angel/devil. It appears that this is the spirit of the marshal that the men of the town have killed and he has returned for justice.

This is the same kind of character that Clint Eastwood portrayed as *The Outlaw Josey Wales* (1976), *Pale Rider* (1985, with its explicit references to the pale rider among the four horsemen of the Apocalypse) and *Unforgiven* (his Oscar-winning film of 1992). These characters are not angels or demons, but they embody the need for a hero who is both angelic and, at least in vengeance, demonic.

Contemporary devils

Cinema audiences are now used to seeing horror-movie demons. They are accompanied by images and symbols from demonology of the past, the medieval gargoyles and the devils that were used to illustrate religious manuscripts. They are also accompanied by a fair amount of 1970s crass language, along with Exorcist-like levitations and bile spewing. There have been plenty of spoofs, like the raucous parody with Leslie Nielsen, *Repossessed*!

But what of more contemporary demons manifesting themselves in our world? More sophisticated demons who are not following Hollywood trends? Two examples, from the 1980s and the 1990s, indicate that the devil can be found anywhere, can be found close to us, either tempting in the manner of the devil testing Jesus in the desert – especially taking him to the top of a high mountain and offering him 'the kingdoms of the earth' – or threatening hell and damnation. The two examples are interesting in so far as the devil is played in *Angel Heart* (1987) by Robert de Niro, calling himself Louis Cyphre (Lucifer) and by Al Pacino in *The Devil's Advocate* (1998), calling himself rather poetically, John Milton, after Paradise Lost.

In *Angel Heart*, De Niro looks both suave and sinister, a

foreigner in New Orleans who is searching for a Big Band singer, Johnny Favorite, who owes him a large debt. He hires a private detective, with the ominous name of Harry Angel, played by Mickey Rourke. The whole plot is ironic because the more that Angel investigates, leaving a trail of death behind him, the deeper he becomes enmeshed in strange voodoo, even satanic rites. At the end of his journey, he does find Johnny Favorite. Favorite is himself. He had sold his soul to the devil for worldly success and Louis Cyphre is using him to do his evil work in repayment. This is the demonic at, one might say, its most diabolical.

The presence of the devil or devils in our world is to lead people astray and destroy them. The archetypal story is that of Dr Faustus, perhaps best known from the plays by Marlowe and Goethe. In the nineteenth century Gounod composed his opera, *Faust*. There was a film version of *Doctor Faustus* in 1967 with Richard Burton as Faust. Istvan Szabo's Oscar-winning film of a German who sold his soul to the Third Reich was called *Mephisto*.

It is said that one of the ways to defeat the devil is to laugh at him. This was done in two versions of *Bedazzled*. In fact, in Stanley Donen's version of 1968, a star vehicle for the comedy of Peter Cook and Dudley Moore, Peter Cook plays the devil, George Spiggott, and Dudley Moore plays the little man, Stanley Moon, who sells his soul for seven wishes. Each time Spiggott outwits Moon by including a condition that Moon did not foresee (like wanting to be forever with his girlfriend and the devil changing them both into nuns!). In one of the sequences, the screenplay humorously but tellingly explains why Lucifer rebelled against God. He sits on a London post box and tells Stanley to keep circling it saying, 'You are wonderful, you are marvellous...' ad infinitum. After a very short time Stanley complains that this is boring. Spiggott agrees and then tells him that this was what angels had to do for God. It was boring, so he suggested, 'Let's change places'. This kind of humour is less to the fore in the 2000 remake by Harold

Ramis with Brendan Fraser as the victim of the devil who, in more equal rights times, is played by Elizabeth Hurley.

There is no lack of reminders of the devil's work in tempting and trapping. With *The Devil's Advocate*, we are in a much more familiar world than that of *Angel Heart*. This is the world of American law, Manhattan, where the role of the law is to make money through all means possible and where defending the guilty is an art form. John Milton presides over the firm, head-hunting savvy young lawyers, especially if they have beautiful and charming wives.

John Milton is a devil that audiences can more readily understand. There is little difficulty in thinking of the legal profession as devilish. While de Niro was smooth and often pictured sitting in an antique chair that gave the impression of being a throne, Pacino is his usual intense self. He is an actor who can rant and rave better than most. Here he has more than ample opportunity. But, the story is not his. It is the story of a young Florida attorney, Kevin Lomax played by Keanu Reeves.

As the screenplay unfolds, Lomax is defending a child abuser. In the washroom, during a break, his conscience is challenged: how can he defend such offenders? But he is also approached by a talent scout for the New York firm. Despite his mother's warnings against going, he and his wife, Mary Ann (Charlize Theron) go to New York, are given a lavish apartment, social standing, headline and lucrative cases. It is Mary Ann who first feels the evil. She is ultimately assaulted by Milton in a church and then kills herself. Lomax likes the life despite his wife's anxiety. Finally, he discovers Milton's identity, learns that he is Milton's son (which is why his mother warned him not to accept the job) and that he has a half-sister. Milton's intention is that they conceive and give birth to the Antichrist. There are tour-de-force sequences as Milton shouts his plans from the rooftops and then, in a boardroom, a wall panel sculpture of hell comes to life culminating in Milton surrounded by flames. Lomax refuses and kills himself.

If *The Devil's Advocate* were to finish at this point, it would be a millennial parable about selling one's soul, about gaining the whole world but losing one's life. However, it does not end here. *The Devil's Advocate* is a kind of *It's a Wonderful Life* in reverse. The head-hunter in the washroom at the beginning of the film, was a demon showing Kevin Lomax not what a miserable world it would be without him, but what a wonderful life he could have if he made a bargain with the devil. As he shoots himself in New York, Lomax finds himself back in that Florida washroom. In the light of what the devil has shown him, his options are now open. Will he be tempted? He does the right thing and goes back into the courtroom with intentions of integrity. As he enters, he is accosted by a reporter who wants an interview and offers fame… The reporter turns into Milton.

It is interesting to see that in 1947, in the immediate post-war era, Hollywood used an angel to prevent a man from succumbing to despair because the world would have been a different and uglier world without him. Fifty years later, Hollywood uses the devil to tempt a man into succumbing to visions of success, luxury and reputation to prevent him from contributing to a decent world of values.

A rather bold and spectacular attempt to portray angels and demons on screen was *Constantine* (2005). Its premise was that the spear which pierced Jesus' side on Calvary had a power for good but was abused by powers of evil (the latest being Hitler!). In fact, the earth was populated by angels and demons, the demons trying to break through into our world, the angels (especially Gabriel) having power to protect humans. Keanu Reeves is the hero. As a troubled boy with visions of the other world, he killed himself but was permitted to come back. He had his own power: to exorcise demons. Finally the devil himself appears to taunt Constantine – but, as it should, goodness prevails.

And so we are back to the beginning of this chapter with Denzel Washington in *Fallen* (1998). Again, on the eve of the millennium, a story of a fallen angel, desperate to stay on earth, but destined to move from one person to another, shifting simply by a touch, to take possession of the soul of the men and women it encounters to destroy them. For those who really want the defeat of the devil, especially at the turn of the millennium, it is there in a mighty battle in church in which a former New York cop has to save the world from the antichrist at five minutes to midnight, 31 December 1999 – the rest of the world can rightly ask why everything has to happen at US East Coast time when it has been 1 January 2000 without much harm being done in the Pacific, Australia, Asia and Europe. The ex-cop is, appropriately, Arnold Schwarzenegger confronting a monstrously large devil, like a new St Michael the Archangel, in *End of Days*!

Sermons on the evils of temptation do not rate highly in our times unless the preacher is a charismatic speaker or is a media-evangelist. However, devil movies are watched by millions and audiences can be challenged as to what they believe about the demonic in our world and in their lives.

A postscript on heaven and hell

Some films take us from this world to the next, into heaven and hell. However, it should be noted that what Christians call judgment and the Catholic teaching of purgatory sometimes find their way into popular movies. For Harry Angel in *Angel Heart*, his quest for the missing singer who turns out to be himself becomes a kind of purgatorial journey. But, it is too late for him. He has already sold his soul to the devil and the film finishes with him descending with Cyphre into hell.

Jim Jarmusch's evocative title for his tale of a young man's grim train journey to a town at the end of the line, *Dead Man* (1996), also suggests a purgatorial experience. After he is shot, he is pursued by three diabolical gunfighters, but is protected by a kind of Indian guardian angel called Nobody. He finally sails in a canoe into the middle of a lake watching the angel and the last gunfighter battle on the shore, destroying each other.

Jacob's Ladder (1991) seems to be a story of the nightmares of a Vietnam veteran, but may be him re-living his life before he finally dies. What are stories of ghosts and hauntings but attempts to grapple with the mystery of life after death and of atonement for evil that the ghosts have committed in their lives? Wasn't that the alarming revelation at the end of *The Sixth Sense* (1999)?

As regards hell, it is always easier to present damnation more vividly than salvation. The frescoes of the Renaissance cathedrals (or the Sistine Chapel) bear witness to this. And, working on the principle of mocking the devil, it is easier to create a comic hell as Woody Allen did in *Deconstructing Harry* (1997). Lightweight but interesting was the elaborate hell with Harvey Keitel reigning supreme and Adam Sandler having to cope with his destiny as his son in *Little Nicky* (2000).

However, a film that is worth seeing in this context, even though it is not a very good film, is Vincent Ward's *What Dreams May Come* (1998). This is the film where Robin Williams' two children are killed in a road accident. His artist wife, Annabella Sciorra, is inconsolable and attempts to kill herself. Then Williams dies, coming to the aid of motorists in trouble. Depressed, his wife does kill herself. The film is Williams' quest to find his wife. When he discovers that her suicide has put her among the damned, he wants to redeem her from hell.

When Williams arrives in heaven, he discovers that it is really a place created out of his own imagination. He finds himself in the midst of some of his wife's paintings, bright and vivid colours and the beauty of nature. His angelic guides in this heaven are in fact his son and daughter in disguise. However, when he discovers that his wife is in hell, he seeks a guide who will take him there to rescue her. She is trapped in a hell formed by her own grim imagination and she does not recognise him. He is prepared to stay in hell for love of her. This self-giving brings her to life and he is able to reunite her with the family.

One of the striking images amongst the visuals of hell that Ward shows us is a kind of sea of faces, a vast ocean-like surface where only the faces of the damned can be seen as they move and gaze upwards without hope. For audiences who do not reflect on whether there is an afterlife or not, for audiences who once believed but have rejected their beliefs, for those who believe but who find it difficult to grasp what heaven or hell are or what they might look like, these film images meet some kind of need to know.

While Jesus himself and biblical writings use frightening and apocalyptic imagery of fire, worms and gnashing of teeth, many say that hell could be ourselves, choosing ourselves and our malice in the face of the good and just God who wishes all people to be saved. Surely, faced in our judgment by this powerful, loving and forgiving God, no one would choose him or herself. They may well be hampered in this choice of God by the burden of evil and sin they have committed during their lives. It may be that the searing light of God has to burn away this evil, so to speak, as intensely as it was committed. Perhaps this is what purgatory means.

There is very little detail in the scriptures of what heaven is like. Two key passages have always been quoted: 'We are God's children now; What shall be has not yet been revealed. We do know that when it is revealed, we shall be like him, for we shall see him as he is' (1 Jn 3:2). 'At present, I know partially; so then I shall know (and love) fully, as I am fully known (and loved). So, faith, hope and love remain, but the greatest of these is love' (1 Cor 13:12-13). Not much for screen images there. Heaven is a matter of the soul and the heart, a loving experience to the full, whatever that may be (or what dreams may come).

CHAPTER 5

Priests on a Pedestal – and Priests Toppled

If you were to glance at the list of actors who have received an Oscar for Best Actor, you might be surprised at the number who have taken on the role of a Catholic priest. Spencer Tracy did it four times, Robert de Niro four times, Bing Crosby three times, Gregory Peck twice and there were single turns by various stars like Jack Lemmon, Jeremy Irons and Henry Fonda. Even Marlon Brando appeared as Cardinal Torquemada, the Grand Inquisitor, in *Christopher Columbus*. The image of the priest has a certain fascination: the blend of the human and the sacred, the down-to-earth with the untouchable, the man who might do good in a world of evil. Well, that may have been the case when Bing Crosby and Barry Fitzgerald ran the parish in the 1944 Best Picture Oscar-winner, *Going My Way*. But is it the image today?

In the last forty years, the status and role of the Catholic priest has drastically changed. Priests used to have important status, even being placed on a pedestal. Since the 1960s, for good reasons and bad, they have been taken off this pedestal. The priesthood has been damaged by widespread scandals of sexual misconduct and sexual abuse of minors, especially in English-speaking countries (and which are beginning to be felt in other parts of the world). Again, the number of priests is dropping. This is true of the western world, the bulk of new vocations to the priesthood coming from Africa and Asia. Large families are generally a thing of the past, so that there are not so many sons available to enter the priesthood as there used to be. The requirement of clerical celibacy means that many men (and parents anxious to have grandchildren) rule out priesthood. Another factor that can deter potential candidates is the excessive pressure placed on active and faithful priests with its concomitant potential for burnout. It is an enormous challenge to be appointed as a Vocations Director to recruit candidates these days.

When considering the role of the priest in modern society, we need to acknowledge that many young people, as well as older 'lapsed' Catholics, do not go to church. Even churchgoers do not feel the old obligation to attend regularly as they used to. They do not actually see many priests, so that their impressions are those formed some time ago and distorted by lack of interest or ignorance or shaped by images from the media, the old rather 'romantic' and 'heroic' image of the priest. Owing to the recent difficulties, this image has turned rather negative.

One way of coming to terms with these perceptions is to re-examine the range of priests seen in the movies, going back to the Golden Years of Hollywood, which we could also call the Golden Years of the movie priest, then tracing the changes, the challenges, the scandals, arriving at the new screen image of the priest. The movies themselves are much more readily available than before, with the range of television channels available as well as videocassettes and DVDs.

In trying to deal with such a vast amount of material, it seems useful to look at four phases: the traditional image of the priest (up to, say, 1960); the raising of questions about the priesthood (1960-70); doubts and scandals (1970 to the present); and new images of the priest (2000 to the present). It also seems prudent to choose significant examples from each phase, like choosing four files or portfolios and taking out helpful samples. They offer the opportunity for readers to look again at the images of priests and attempt some assessment or reassessment.

The traditional image of the priest

Until 1959 Catholics, as well as any movie audience who did not share Catholic beliefs, might have assumed that the images of priests that they saw on the screen would continue in the same vein for forever and a day. But 1959 was the year that Pope John XXIII announced the summoning of a world council which was to review the practice of the Church in all areas. This 'Second Vatican Council' opened in October 1962 and concluded its work in December 1965. The Church would never be the same again.

However, until then the Church had been the same. The image of the priest and the screen image of the priest were the same. This is what people took for granted whether this image appealed to them or not. But who embodied this image? And what was it like?

It needs to be said – because this image is not familiar, and already the people who remember this era are getting much older – that it was taken very seriously. This was how a priest should be. There have been recent movements within the Catholic Church which hark back to these 'good and orthodox' days, especially for the status of the clergy and priests being seen to be priests.

Priests were an integral part of the Church structure. They took their place in the priestly hierarchy of the Church: Pope, bishops, priests, deacons – then members of religious orders and the laity. It is as if they belonged to a hierarchical caste, a clerical caste. Their sense of special vocation, their six to seven years of training in philosophy and theology in the context of an enclosed seminary with a strict regime, their celebration of Mass, their hearing of confessions, their officiating at weddings, their anointing of the sick meant that they were to be holy and edifying men. In fact, the priest was seen as an 'alter Christus', 'another Christ'. The Gospel pattern of Jesus' ministry was meant to be both norm and inspiration.

The priest was distinguished from other men. He wore liturgical vestments. He wore clerical garb: a soutane in the presbytery and church, a clerical suit with Roman collar and hat. His ecclesiastical language was Latin. Priests were also celibate. While this had not always been the case in the Catholic Church, the requirement was instituted in the eleventh century to guard against abuses in sexual behaviour and paying more attention to family finances than to Church business. It had an almost thousand-year tradition. Priests did not marry. Priests have always found the obligation of celibacy a challenge, but priests who broke their vows or who gave up their priesthood disappeared. In the words of one writer, they became 'shepherds in the mist'.

Priesthood was something that had to be lived up to and Catholics had very high expectations of their priests. In fact, they often placed them on a pedestal. The priest was elevated to clerical status, but also to a status that expected him to be more than human. Concessions were made to human weakness, especially in keeping the vow of celibacy, in countries with a more tolerant Hispanic tradition – in Latin America and the Philippines. The concession made by Catholics in Anglo-Celtic cultures, not only in Britain or Ireland, but in the United States and Australia, was that the priest might drink. Many Irish clergy were prodigious drinkers!

So, priests, who generally worked in the structures of a parish, under the authority of the local Bishop who was responsible to central government in Rome, were seen as the religious authority figures to whom Catholics came for opinions, advice and, if they were approachable, for personal and family help and support.

One of the dynamic features of nineteenth century Churches, not just the Catholic Church, was the sending of priests, brothers and sisters to 'foreign missions'. These men and women generally belonged to religious orders that were asked to pioneer the establishing of the Church in lands that had little or no tradition of Christian presence. These men and women were 'sent', as 'missioners', to preach the Gospel. Many made converts, especially in Africa and the Pacific islands. Many of them were killed for their efforts. Many were seen as the religious side of colonising power. Many contributed to the development of nations and, in the twentieth century, many identified closely with the peoples with whom they worked. They became 'acculturated'.

Parish activities and missionary endeavour were represented in the movies up till 1960.

PHASE ONE:
Screen images of the traditional priest

The films of five actors have been chosen to illustrate this phase of priests on screen: Spencer Tracy in *San Francisco* (1936), *Boys' Town* (1938), *Men of Boys' Town* (1939), *The Devil at Four O'clock* (1962); Pat O'Brien in *Angels with Dirty Faces* (1938), *The Fighting 69th* (1940), *Fighting Father Dunne* (1948), *The Fireball* (1951); Bing Crosby in *Going My Way* (1944), *The Bells of St Mary's* (1945), *Say One for Me* (1959); Gregory Peck in *The Keys of the Kingdom* (1944) – he also appeared as a Monsignor helping the interned escape from World War II Italy in *The Scarlet and the Black* (1984); Alec Guinness in *Father Brown Detective* (1954), *The Prisoner* (1955) – he also appeared as Pope Innocent III in *Brother Sun, Sister Moon* (1973) and as *Monsignor Quixote* (1980). It is of interest to note that Tracy, Crosby and Peck all had Catholic upbringing, while Alec Guinness was a convert at the time of making *Father Brown* and *The Prisoner* and remained a devout practising Catholic.

Spencer Tracy

What did Spencer Tracy bring to the screen? Looking older than he actually was, he tended to communicate an air of authority and respectability. This was especially true of his two performances (in his mid to late 30s) as Fr Edward

Flanagan, the founder of the American Boys' Town, the priest who said that he had never met a bad boy. In fact, Fr Flanagan (as one of the principal screen images of the priest during the 1930s) seems to represent the norm for what a priest should be like. He was a man of integrity. That was taken for granted. He was a man of conviction. He fully exemplified all the requirements of the priest. He looked and acted like a priest. Besides being a man of conviction, he was a man of zeal. Spencer Tracy looked like 'another Christ' as he sought out boys who were homeless, wayward, hopeless cases, and gave them a home. He became a father figure. Fr Flanagan was the down-to-earth, practical and pragmatic American pastor, someone that anyone, Catholic or not, could look up to, admire and emulate. Spencer Tracy's appeal to the American public and box-office was at its strongest at this time. He won two Oscars for Best Actor, for *Captains Courageous* in 1937 and for Fr Flanagan in *Boys' Town* in 1938.

Spencer Tracy's first performance as a priest, Fr Tim Mullin in *San Francisco*, showed yet another side of this vocation: to be a buddy, a best friend. In this film Clark Gable played Blackie Norton, a variation on his frequent, debonair screen character, more at home with the world and the flesh. While Hollywood has always liked the devil, this was the period of the strict Motion Picture Code, and film producers preferred an angelic presence to a diabolical one. Fr Mullin was a guardian angel. He was Norton's best friend, his buddy, the pal who had made good while Norton chose the slippery path. He served as conscience and moral challenge. When disaster struck in the form of the famous 1906 earthquake, Fr Mullin also demonstrated the self-sacrificing heroic side of his character and his priesthood. This was a priest that men could admire, the priest as a man's man but one who could also reassure women. He was in touch with the world, but was not worldly.

When Tracy's fourth film as a priest was released in 1962, *The Devil at Four O'clock*, a quarter of a century had passed. The movies could be a little franker in their presentations of priests as human beings. This is a missionary film (set in Tahiti). Tracy's Fr Doolan is a good man, but is a drinker (as was Tracy himself). He confronts four escaped convicts (among them Frank Sinatra) and challenges their stances. The priest is still a hero, but he has visible and recognisable weaknesses, an indication that the films of the 1960s would not simply show the good priest.

Pat O'Brien

Another actor who portrayed several priests in this period was Pat O'Brien, once again a Catholic himself. The films he appeared in as a priest were not as up-market as those of Spencer Tracy. Instead, he showed the B-side of the Catholic priest, the tough boy who went straight, the military chaplain, the do-gooder pioneer and crusader. He epitomised the down-to-earth priest in the inner city who, as in *Angels with Dirty Faces* (1938), went on to ordination instead of taking the gangster path that his school friend, played by James Cagney, took to execution. He was a Fr Flanagan of *Hell's Kitchen* (1939) in helping the Bowery Boys keep on the right side of the law.

The Fighting 69th (1940) was made in the first year of World War II, but before America became involved. O'Brien is the chaplain, Fr Duffy, who again has to deal with Cagney as Jerry Plunkett, who has a coward's streak that could lead to disaster and loss of life. This was the same year that O'Brien portrayed famed Notre Dame football coach, Knute Rockne, with his famous line to player, Ronald Reagan, 'Do it for the Gipper'. O'Brien was Everyman's chaplain and coach. He was to appear as a priest twice more, again in low-budget films. Each time he emulated the ministry of Tracy's Fr Flanagan. He played the title role in *Fighting Father Dunne* (1948). The film was set in 1905 with Fr Peter Dunne championing the newsboys, trying to set up a co-op orphanage to give them a home base as well as some mediation in their struggles with the bosses. O'Brien met up with Spencer

Tracy's chief boy in *Boys' Town*, Mickey Rooney, in the short feature, *The Fireball* (1951). This time he is Fr O'Hara who runs the orphanage that Rooney runs away from.

O'Brien is not so well remembered these days, except for *Angels with Dirty Faces*. However, in his time, in a more modest way than the big stars, he embodied the priest who was not afraid to get his hands dirty in a committed ministry to difficult characters.

Bing Crosby

Bing Crosby represented the good priest. His Fr O'Malley, *Going My Way* (1944) like Tracy's Fr Flanagan, won him an Oscar as Best Actor (with Barry Fitzgerald's old Fr Fitzgibbon winning Best Supporting Actor) – indicating once again the tolerance of American moviegoers during World War II, who were pleased with this kind of priest on screen and paid to see him.

Going My Way and its immediate sequel, *The Bells of St Mary's* (1945), were pieces of religious whimsy. They took for granted the traditional American Catholicism of the late nineteenth century and the early twentieth century. Fr Fitzgibbon had built his church in 1898 and was still parish priest 45 years later. He was Irish and a stickler for clerical dress, rubrics and regulations for prayer. Fr O'Malley, on the other hand, was the new breed of confident priests in the increasingly large Catholic Church. They were American. They exhibited enthusiasm in ministry, an outgoing American friendliness, a less immediately judgmental attitude towards 'sinners', a human clerical face. They were as devout and as faithful as the preceding generations of priests, but they wore their dignity more lightly. (In twenty years time they would be the middle-aged generation who would have to deal with the changes of the Second Vatican Council and help the ordinary faithful to understand and accept those changes.)

For a while, in the 1960s and 1970s, many Catholics found *Going My Way* and *The Bells of St Mary's* rather irritating. They thought it smacked of complacency in a Church that was about to disappear, that Crosby's character trivialised the priesthood, that as a priest he was not deep enough. After all, he did marriage counselling simply sitting at a piano and crooning 'Aren't you going my way too?' His pastoral outreach was to accompany kids singing the Oscar-winning song of the year, 'Swinging on a star'! In *The Bells of St Mary's* he did have to face up to some tough issues, especially sparring with Ingrid Bergman as Sister Benedict, the principal of the parish school. Nowadays, we can see *Going My Way* in greater historical perspective, as showing a more genial face of the Church, a sympathetic priest for more straightforward times.

Bing Crosby appeared once more as a priest in a showbiz story, *Say One for Me* (1959). His Fr Conroy may be Fr O'Malley fifteen years on, a chaplain to the show business community and spending a lot of time helping out the daughter of a friend (played by Debbie Reynolds) who is dancing in a club of dubious reputation. Fr Conroy also solves everyone's problems and shows his singing talents as he puts on a benefit. Perhaps this was more Hollywood than Church, something 'feel good' in widescreen and colour just before everything began to change.

Gregory Peck

In only his second film, *The Keys of the Kingdom* (1944), Gregory Peck took the image of the screen priest beyond the United States. He and Vincent Price portrayed missionary priests in China in the early twentieth century. China was a popular country for missionaries both Protestant and Catholic. Peck, at the time the film was made, was in his late twenties. The earliest age a priest could normally be ordained at this time was twenty-four.

While Rev. Angus Mealey, the missionary portrayed by Vincent Price, flourished in his mission, Gregory Peck's Fr Chisholm experiences great struggles in his ministry. This is the human/heroic portrait of the priest who is completely dedicated and detached from worldly goods and success. He lives his life of celibacy, feels a sense of failure in his work because of few converts and experiences hardships in the lives of the people he is evangelising, their poverty, hunger and overwhelming natural disasters. This is the ideal priest, the priest that most people know they could never be, who is prepared for a life of self-sacrifice and who is willing to die for his people and his mission. He is the living martyr. He is most certainly an 'alter Christus'. This is the priest at his sincere best, a man of authenticity and integrity.

The Keys of the Kingdom was firmly based on the novel from which it was adapted, written by celebrated and prolific Scottish author, A.J. Cronin. Another novel, *The Citadel,* had already been filmed in 1938 starring Robert Donat and *The Green Years* was about to be filmed. Cronin also provided the stories for television's *Doctor Finlay's Casebook.*

By the mid-1940s, Hollywood had provided substantial priestly images: the pioneer, the pastor, and the missionary. The other strong image of the priest in this period came from Britain in the films of Alec Guinness.

Alec Guinness

Unfortunately Alec Guinness played G.K. Chesterton's parish priest-detective, *Father Brown Detective* (1954), only once. It would have made an entertaining series as he sought out the master criminal, Flambeau (Peter Finch) who disguised himself as a priest among a group of English clergy going on a pilgrimage to Rome, but who gave himself away to Fr Brown by not realising that he had eaten a meat sandwich on Friday. Fr Brown had more than a touch of bumbling, much to the irritation of his bishop, the blustering Cecil Parker, but he was a man who obviously loved God, was devoted to his parish ministry, preaching a worthy sermon on lost sheep and forgiveness, and combining an ability to move in aristocratic circles with sheer ordinariness.

However, it was his role in *The Prisoner* (1955) that contributed another screen image of the priest in this era of Church stability and tradition. The film was based on a play by Bridget Boland, recounting the experiences of the Hungarian Catholic primate, Cardinal Josef Mindszenty.

The 1950s was the period when the Cold War between the United States and its allies and the Soviet Union and its allies froze. It was a period of fierce anti-Communism in America, with the danger of nuclear threats that were to come to the surface and world awareness in the early 1960s. It was the period of 'Un-American Activities' and the drastic investigations by Senator McCarthy. It was the period of migration from the countries of Eastern Europe. It was also, especially under President Eisenhower (1953-1960), the period of the prosperous American dream.

Because of the blacklisting of alleged Communist sympathisers in government and in the film industry, there were a great many propaganda films. Already in 1950, Cardinal Mindszenty's arrest, interrogation and imprisonment (soon to be repeated for Church leaders in Czechoslovakia, Poland, Ukraine and the Baltic countries) had been the subject of a small-budget film, extensively seen by Catholic groups, *Guilty of Treason* (1950), starring Charles Bickford as the Cardinal.

The Prisoner did not emerge from the American anti-Communist experience, but it does reflect the apprehensions of the 1950s. Its portrait of a cardinal, the victim of a totalitarian regime, offered a new kind of martyr priest. Jack Hawkins is the government 'Interrogator' who knows how to capitalise on physical deprivation by applying psychological pressure. This was the era of concern about brainwashing, something that came to the fore in the Korean War (dramatically captured in the film version of Richard Condon's *The Manchurian Candidate* where it was exploited by right-wing pressure groups against the American government, the film being released in the year before John F. Kennedy's assassination).

In *The Prisoner* Alec Guinness is the Cardinal, a prince of the Church, reinforcing the horror for Catholics of those days that a dignitary of the hierarchy should be so humiliated and persecuted. The Cardinal himself is a good man, a good priest. However, he has his human failings, something that the interrogator is able to exploit by trying to destroy the Cardinal's self-confidence, self-image and faith. While this is in no way shocking now, it was a jolt to religious audiences of the 50s to realise that a priest and a cardinal could be afflicted by human weakness or sinfulness. This was edging the priest off his pedestal. Since it was done by anti-religious forces, it was despised and the priest-victim became a martyr and his weaknesses exonerated. This was noble thinking and feeling, but it was also unrealistic. Within a few years, the Church would change and the traditional image of the priest would be questioned and challenged.

It is important to add as a postscript to this phase one more images of the priest: Karl Malden's Fr Barry in *On the Waterfront* (1954). Budd Schulberg's screenplay puts impressive speeches into Fr Barry's mouth. He is a priest in a New York waterfront parish. With the corruption in union leadership on the docks, including murder, he is challenged to take a stand against injustice. His sermons are fiery for justice. His final speech to the men, where he speaks of the suffering of Jesus and his way of the cross while Terry Molloy (Marlon Brando) who has been badly beaten but stands to defy the brutal bullies, is a reminder that the church is not just there to provide parishes for comfortable suburbanites, but that Jesus preached a message of justice for all.

During this phase, ministers and pastors from other churches were represented generally in the context of their parish work. If Barry Fitzgerald provided screen priests from *Going My Way* to *The Quiet Man*, his brother, Arthur Shields, was frequently a reverend. Significant ministers from this period include Fredric March in *One Foot in Heaven* (1941), Richard Todd as Peter Marshall in *A Man Called Peter* (1954) and Don Murray as the celebrated Norman Vincent Peale in *One Man's Way* (1961).

Questioning the image and the reality

The 1960s was a decade of extraordinarily rapid change in behaviour and attitudes, especially in the Western world. However, it was also a decade of revolutionary change in Africa with the throwing off of colonialism, a decade of unrest in Latin America, and a decade of war in South-East Asia.

Freedom and freedoms were the order of the day. The 1960s began with the enthusiasm of the Kennedy era. The drug culture was soon to emerge with its accompanying hippy movement and the drug-taking of the troops in Vietnam. Sexual freedom had been talked about, but was now more openly practised. It was the age of the pill. On the religious level, there was critique of traditional expressions of theology with Bishop John Robinson achieving some notoriety early in the decade with his critique of religious understanding, 'Honest to God', and with Paul Tillich and other philosopher-theologians arguing for a moratorium on the use of the word 'God'. (It was at this time that the Catholic Church changed its translation of the Jewish scriptures from 'God' to 'Yahweh'.) At Easter, 1966, *Time Magazine* published a cover story – in black with a red border – asking 'Is God Dead?'.

The response of the Catholic Church, pioneered by the foresight of Pope John XXIII in calling the Second Vatican Council as early as January 1959, was three years of preparation and four years of actual deliberations by the Council. It was a re-think of the vocation and ministry of the church, looking for 'signs of the times' (one of the favourite phrases of the Council) which would lead both to renewal and updating.

Because the questions had been asked, it was possible to give more than one answer to these questions. Included in this new agenda was the role of the priest in a changing understanding of the church. The principal document from the Council considered the nature of the Church, *Lumen Gentium* (Light of the Nations, a quotation from the book of

Isaiah, 42:10, where the prophet, in whom God delights, is described as a light of the nations and covenant of the peoples, whose ministry is quiet, gentle and persuasive, not hurting any bruised reed, not extinguishing even a smouldering wick.) There was also a document on the priesthood.

If the Church was now to be seen according to the image of the servant of God, for the people of God (another favourite Council phrase), the priest must be seen as a servant, involved in sacred duties, but also to be seen 'with' the people rather than above them. The pedestal was not an image of the Council. The priest would be helped in his changing role by liturgy in the vernacular of the people, a reconsideration of the ministry of the sacraments and the involvement of the Church in the 'Modern World' (the title of another of the Council's major documents). While continuity with tradition was to be taken for granted, this continuity had to be creative and adapted to the needs of the times.

This change of perspective on priesthood had enormous consequences for the developing relationships between priests and people. Most embraced the changes (some more slowly than others). Others resisted. Thousands made alternative choices, especially when clerical celibacy could be questioned despite firm rulings that it should stay in place, and left the priesthood. Others experimented sexually, leading double lives. By 1970, the face of the church had changed drastically from what it looked like in 1960.

PHASE TWO:

Screen images of the traditional priest

The Cardinal

While there had been some challenge to the traditional image of the priesthood in the movies, including some suggestions of sexual troubles, the 'Thorn Birds' syndrome', in very early films like *The Church and the Woman* (Australia, 1917), the screen image of the priest up to 1960 was mostly very edifying. In 1947 John Ford had adapted Graham Greene's novel *The Power and the Glory,* the story of the Mexican whisky priest and his moral choices in relationships and in accepting the political consequences and danger to life in his serving the poor. It was renamed *The Fugitive* (1943) starring Henry Fonda. It was considered a watered-down version of Greene's powerful novel. Audiences were not ready for the full impact of this story and its implications in the 1940s (and, besides, it was set in Mexico). American television networks decided that its audiences were ready for a new version, calling it by its original title and starring Laurence Olivier as the priest (1962).

For cinema audiences worldwide, it was Otto Preminger's *The Cardinal* (1963) that first broached alternative possibilities for the priest. The novel, by Henry Morton Robinson, had been popular reading, a bestseller, for many Catholics. It fitted the changing climate in thinking about priesthood. The other popular novel with a tormented priest (who remained faithful even though he came to realise that his bureaucratic life in the Vatican had turned him into a desiccated man and priest) was Morris West's *The Devil's Advocate* (1961) which was not filmed until 1977, with John Mills in the central role, when its impact and surprise value came too late to the screen.

The picture of the priesthood in *The Cardinal* was both down-to-earth and worldly-wise. Tom Tryon portrays the Boston priest who is sent by his Cardinal (John Huston doing something of an impersonation of the then Archbishop of Boston and confidant of the Kennedy clan, Cardinal Richard Cushing) out to the back blocks where he works with a good priest who has been neglected by the diocese (Burgess Meredith). As a student in Rome, he catches the eye of a sympathetic bishop (Raf Vallone) and is eventually offered a post in the Vatican. So far, so normal, except that

Preminger's big-budget movie was given the blockbuster treatment. *The Cardinal* was a big film, with name stars, publicised for the widest audience possible.

Perhaps the most sensational aspect of *The Cardinal* in retrospect is not that the priest needs to reconsider his vocation and take time off (soon to become a commonplace with priests in the 1970s), but that in his visit to Georgia and his promoting the social justice teaching of the Church, he is taken by the Ku Klux Klan and whipped by them in front of the burning cross. You didn't see that kind of thing, that kind of heroism in the movies up till then.

The Cardinal was screened in Rome in 1963 for the bishops attending the second session of the Vatican council. Preminger himself was honoured with a Papal medal from Pope Paul VI and may well have been surprised by the endorsement of his film by the church.

The Cardinal presaged what was to come. Tom Tryon's priest becomes unsure in his vocation despite his fine Boston Catholic family, the best seminary education, pastoral experience of the demanding type and the prestige of his Vatican job. Within five years, many Catholics would be asking why these credentials were not enough for a man to be firmly committed to his priestly vocation. Why would he consider leaving the priesthood? Weren't taking his vow of celibacy and his vow of obedience to his Bishop sufficient to give him the moral strength to persevere? In *The Cardinal* they are not enough to eliminate doubts. He needs time by himself, time to be a man, time for some anonymity. He also experiences the need to risk falling in love and breaking his vows. Perhaps the audience of bishops at the 1963 Vatican screening heaved a collective sigh of relief at the scene where the cardinal finally meets the woman who does not know the man she is in love with is a priest, turns to her and is wearing a Roman collar. While she is disappointed, she seems to take it in fairly good grace. But, in fact, it was a sign of things to come – and rapidly so.

Another 'prophetic' feature of *The Cardinal* was the sub-plot about the cardinal's sister and her difficult pregnancy. Until 1963, screen priests – except if they were in a Graham Greene movie: besides *The Fugitive*, priests appeared briefly, but theologically tellingly, in *The Heart of the Matter* (1952) and *The End of the Affair* (1955) – did not have to exercise their minds with difficult moral issues like those they studied for four years in the Moral Theology textbooks and their case studies, which had the luxury of theoretical debate rather than actual pastoral practice. As the family, and their son priest, gather at the hospital, the mother is in danger of losing her life in childbirth. Should the child die to save the mother? Should the mother die to save the child? What was easy to say in theory was far more difficult to say in practice. The mother dies.

The emotional dimension of such tragedies in moral dilemmas was always present, but there was a Catholic stoicism that tended to get people through the problems at the time. With such a widescreen dramatic presentation of this issue, the way was open to explore moral theology both intellectually and emotionally. Since the 1970s American telemovies and episodes of series have thrived on such scenarios. Watching a movie is predominantly an emotional experience – which has led to a home audience that is emotionally savvy while far less intellectually savvy.

The Exorcist

It was the sometimes acerbic reviewer for *The New Yorker*, the celebrated Pauline Kael, who remarked that *The Exorcist* (1973) was the biggest poster pro the Catholic Church since *The Bells of St Mary's*. Others commented at the time, when the hype about the movie being a terrifying experience was rampant, that Catholics who believed may not have liked the special effects, but had no difficulty with the religious themes. Non-believers would treat it as just another horror movie and take it or leave it. Those who, like Ellen Burstyn's mother of the possessed Regan, had lapsed in their practice, would be the ones who found it most difficult. They were brought up in belief and so the events on screen could be real, that there was a devil and a hell.

The Exorcist was based on events that occurred in Georgetown, Washington DC, in 1949 (portrayed with more accuracy, but less flair in the 2000 film *The Possessed* with Timothy Dalton). It was only because of changes in what was allowed to be seen on screen in the 1970s that the movie could be made.

It should be said immediately that the two priests in *The Exorcist* are very good priests and are portrayed with dignity and insight by Max Von Sydow and Jason Miller. What was unusual at this stage (perhaps hard to understand for audiences brought up on *The Omen* and countless other diabolical possession movies) was seeing this kind of role for priests. Possession is not an everyday experience and seeing two devout men desperately praying, going through rituals of blessings and holy water sprinklings and being foully abused by the possessed girl, made audiences ask questions about the priesthood, the kind of dedication and commitment required for such emotionally and spiritually arduous work, especially as it resulted in injury and, finally, death. In one sense, it restored some appreciation of the priesthood. In another, it seemed to relegate the priest to a world of esoteric beliefs and behaviour.

Movie buffs who saw Ken Russell's *The Devils* (1970) would have had these attitudes reinforced. In that film about religious hysteria in Loudun, France, in 1634, a sexually repressed group of women, forced by their families and poverty to enter a convent, seem to be possessed by devils. They are exorcised in staged rituals for the benefit of Cardinal Richelieu so that his troops can enter the city on the pretext of restoring order and so take charge of Loudun. It is the trappings of Catholicism gone berserk. In the midst of all this mayhem, the most serene character is the Jesuit, Fr Grandier (Oliver Reed), who is the nun's confessor and object of desire. He has gone through a ritual of marriage with a woman from the city and is ultimately burned at the stake, a truer priest and martyr than those involved in the farcical hysteria.

Other priests were seen in the spate of horror dramas of diabolical activity that followed in the 1970s and into the 1980s and 90s (*Exorcist II*, with Richard Burton as the priest in 1976, *Exorcist III* as late as 1990), making audiences wonder what exactly priests did, while Catholics who retained the traditional image of the priest were puzzled over what was happening, e.g. *The Sentinel* (1977), *The Amityville Horror* (1979), *Amityville II: The Possession* (1982).

True Confessions

One might say that this is a daft title for a strong film that offers some of the best images for gauging what was happening to the priesthood on screen and in real life and what some of the key questions really were. *True Confessions* (1981) was not a film in the popular gossip magazine or true romance style – although audiences might have wondered as the film opened with a parish priest dying of a heart attack in a brothel. By 1980, merely fifteen years after the end of Vatican II, movies were offering images vastly different from *Going My Way*. This is not 'nice' material, but it is challenging.

The setting is Los Angeles. The time is 1948. In one way this distances the action from criticism of the contemporary Church but, of course, that's what it is. Through the strength and intelligence of the writing (John Gregory Dunne adapted his novel with his wife, screenwriter, Joan Didion) and the performances of Robert de Niro and Robert Duvall as two brothers, the film stands out as a thoughtful examination of a diocese and, especially, of a high-profiled priest's vocational commitment and crisis.

Cyril Cusack plays the Cardinal Archbishop of Los Angeles as a lordly prelate of the times, shrewd in management and somewhat devious in politics (trying to get rid of the diocesan builder involved in some sordid behaviour by honouring him as Catholic layman of the year and, after he is placed so strongly in the public eye, firing him). But it is Robert de Niro, as the Chancellor of the diocese, Fr Des Spellacy, who has the central role. He plays him as a good man caught up in the day-to-day administration as well as the long-term planning. This gives him time for little else, pastorally speaking as well as for his life of prayer. He has succeeded, despite taunts from his journalist brother (Duvall), who is doing investigative reporting on the diocese, seeking the rather too many skeletons in the cupboard.

Eventually Fr Spellacy has to face himself, his conscience and God. He is in danger of becoming a worldly priest. He retires to the desert. When his brother visits him, he is able to confess to him. His life has become a life of repentance and atonement. His crisis has led him to salvation. This is a perennial issue for those priests who spend their time in offices, in tribunals, in business meetings, as well as those priests who are involved in a ministry that is not face-to-face in a parish, school or hospital. It is the issue of 'what exactly is priestly work?' If a person is not involved in this face-to-face ministry, why be a priest?

By 1980, many priests were working in ministries that were not directly linked to parishes. Some lectured in universities, some high-flyers were advisers to finance corporations, some were employed by the increasing number of charity and justice organisations. While Paul VI was Pope, it was not so difficult for a priest in crisis to apply to the Vatican for reconsideration of his ordination, to examine whether there had been full consent to being ordained. If there had been pressure or some immaturity in decision-making, a dispensation from the obligations of priesthood was granted. After the accession of Pope John Paul II, Vatican officials took a sterner stance. It was said that a priest would not be dispensed. This was not accurate. Rather, the brief presenting the case for 'laicisation' had to be more detailed and thorough than was previously required. Many priests decided not to wait for their case to be considered, left the priesthood and married. Others felt that the questioning was too intrusive and left.

It is worth noting one of the insights of the time, especially as a number of priests left their ministry soon after a parent, especially a mother, died. It was a commonplace to remark that a mother had a vocation, not the son. But, many fine young men, with exemplary Catholic parents, decided not to go on. It was not overt pressure from the parents that made the young man enter a seminary, rather the young man wanted to do the best he could in life for his parents and concluded that the best way would be to become a priest. It was only later that these men realised that they did not have a vocation to the priesthood.

It was in this context that *True Confessions* was released. The significant thing about De Niro's priest was that he fully considered the role of his priesthood and his commitment to it. And it led him out of the diocese, into the desert where he could, in a more humble and poor lifestyle, be an authentic priest. *True Confessions* raised the issues of authenticity and integrity in a complicated life and opted for the priest simplifying his life in full commitment.

Scandals, midsconduct and abuse

In the 1980s very few priests would have expected that, a decade later and, especially for the United States' clergy in 2002, they would spend so much time at meetings concerning sexual scandals and abuse. They had little idea of how much the revelations of the 1990s would impact on the members of the Church, creating shock, denial, anger. They had little idea of how many men and women would come forward to make official complaints to Church authorities. They could not anticipate the extent and depth of apology that would be asked of the Church and how difficult the hierarchies would find it to express their sorrow and regret and ask forgiveness. They had little idea of how many court cases would be held, how many priests would go to jail and the enormous sums of money that would be paid to victims with incalculable impact on the variety of Church activities that had depended on those funds and how the faithful would become more cautious in their giving of money for Church works. But this is what happened.

Sexual abuse is not confined to clergy or church workers. Information that has emerged in recent decades indicates that abuse of children is far more widespread than most people imagined, especially in families. Even during the 1980s, most people did not think of going to the police in these cases. They felt that they had to deal with them privately. One of the tasks that occupied people of all institutions dealing with children during the 1990s, especially Church institutions, was the preparations of protocols and codes of behaviour so that institutions could act properly with regard to complainants and victims as well as not pre-judging those accused. This is still a matter of delicacy within the Churches. In most countries, it has been agreed that matters go to the police.

Where it is not immediately a police matter, accused clergy are asked to step down from their ministry until the inquiry is completed. Some ecclesiastical authorities think this is too drastic a measure and leads to injustice for those who have been falsely accused. The American scandals of 2002 made people realise how widespread misconduct and abusive behaviour has been and how difficult it is, especially in such a litigious culture as the United States, to ensure immediate justice for all parties. While the sex scandals in the Church have been principally in English-speaking countries, more revelations have been made in Western Europe and South Africa. One expects that within the next few years, there will be complaints from Africa and Asia.

While many people were shocked as well as dismayed by the acknowledgement that so many priests had not lived up to their vow of celibacy (while preaching purity from the pulpit), stories of affairs between consenting adults have been a recurring aspect of the history of the priesthood. Stories of sexual misconduct, sexual behaviour as well as harassment now began to emerge. It is fair to say that revelations about the abuse of children were particularly scandalous.

By 2000, with the world celebrating the new millennium and the Church celebrating the Jubilee Year, the image of the clergy was very low in many parts of the world, statistics for the number of priests worldwide being boosted by Africa and Asia. Apart from families being smaller and the number of men available for priesthood decreasing, and apart from the requirement of celibacy being maintained, the image of the priest had become something of a negative one. Newspaper articles featured the accused and gave information about convicted clergy. Radio talkback never tired of the subject. Television coverage in the news magazine programmes as well as documentary specials provided not just words but images of the people concerned – and television is a medium for emotions. Information is perennially (and immediately) available on Internet websites.

The first made-for-TV movie about the sexual scandals was produced by Home Box Office in 1990. It was called *Judgment* and was based on the first reported scandal in the United States, in Louisiana. It had a strong cast with Keith Carradine and Blythe Danner as the parents of the abused boy. David Strathairn played the priest, Fr Auburn, with Bob Gunton as the Vicar General and William Windom as the Bishop. The storyline follows the events surrounding the molestation of several young boys, including initial disbelief on the part of the parents, and the desperate attempts of the Church establishment to cover up the misdeeds and admit no culpability.

PHASE THREE:
The scandalous screen priest

Priest

It was provocative, of course, of the distributors of the BBC movie, *Priest,* to release it in the United States on St Patrick's

Day 1995. When what might now be called 'religious terrorists' threw bombs into New Jersey cinemas screening the film, it was clear that the movie had offended some of the public whether they had seen it or not. The Catholic League initiated a campaign against the movie and Cardinal O'Connor of New York felt able to rely on trusted reviewers, rather than seeing the film himself, to declare that it was as bad as anything that had 'rotted on the silver screen'. Reactions to the movie in Europe and other parts of the world were more judicious. OCIC (the International Catholic Organisation for Cinema) issued a press release on the film that was read publicly by the bishop responsible for the media in Germany at an Ecumenical service during the Berlin Film Festival where the film was screened. *Priest* was then shown to priests in Germany where they could discuss the film, its worth and its impact on audiences. A number of other Bishops' conferences followed suit. *Priest* became *the* film to see during 1995 in the light of what was happening to priests and their image.

Priest began its life as a modest television film for the BBC, written by Catholic author, Jimmy McGovern, who had recently moved back to the Church following the death of his father and was appreciative of the help given by the priests at that sad time. McGovern was interested in the role of priests in the 1990s, the issues of celibacy and of sexual orientation and the role of confession and its protection of secrecy for the privacy of the penitent. Although the setting was Liverpool, Archbishop Derek Worlock preferred that churches in the city not be used for shooting the film, so an Anglican church in London served as substitute. Director Antonia Bird, brought up Anglican, did research in Liverpool, being welcomed to Mass by the priests with whom she discussed the project. *Priest* was intended as a contemporary story of priesthood in 1990s England. It should be said that child abuse issues had only just begun to surface in Britain and Ireland at the time *Priest* was filmed and released. The child abuse issue in the film took place in a Catholic home, a father victimising his daughter.

Quite a number of characters in the film were priests. In fact, it opened with an angry priest charging the window of the Bishop's residence with a large crucifix! The Bishop was not a sympathetic character, preferring to simply get rid of difficult priests than do anything substantial for them except to send them to the fringes of the diocese to live with older judgmental priests who conversed in Latin.

The two central priests raised the celibacy issues very clearly. The parish priest was a zealous man who had spent time in Latin America as a missionary. On his return to Liverpool, he was conscious of his experience abroad, that a man was expected to be with a woman otherwise he was not truly a man. He was living in his presbytery with his housekeeper in what was formerly and technically called 'concubinage'. This came as a shock and a scandal to his new assistant, Fr Greg Pilkington (Linus Roache), one of the group of more traditional young men being ordained in the 1990s. He, however, was tormented by his homosexual orientation. He spends the night with a man he meets at a club, then refuses him communion at Mass. When he meets him again, he is arrested for lewd behaviour, is shamed and attempts suicide. In the meantime, he has become concerned about a young girl whose confession he hears and who reveals abuse by her father. He is overwhelmed and, in a very moving scene, prays desperately before the crucifix about God's seeming inaction in painful experiences. He wants a miraculous intervention. He does not realise it but, because of a dispute at a parish meeting, he ends it early, enabling the mother to return home earlier than expected and to discover what was happening.

Fr Greg brought to the screen for the first time in a major film the issue of a priest's sexual orientation, something that was discussed during the 1990s by the Churches. The basic principle of a priest leading a celibate life no matter what his orientation had been a long tradition in the Church, although one that had not been openly acknowledged in many countries. With fewer vocations to priesthood in the Catholic Church, quite a number of men attracted to the celibate priesthood are men with a homosexual orientation.

During the questioning times of the late 1960s and 1970s, a number of priests, in the United States for instance, took the line that, since marriage was not involved, they were not breaking their vows in same-sex partnerships. The AIDS epidemic took its toll among some clergy, an issue that has not been widely discussed. With the more recent problems concerning homosexual clergy and bishops in the Anglican Communion, more controversy can be expected.

The finale of *Priest* is highly emotional. Fr Greg comes back to the parish to ask the people's forgiveness for his behaviour and the scandal. He joins the parish priest to concelebrate the Mass. Offended parishioners shout abuse and walk out, some quoting the scriptures in a harshly unforgiving way. Fr Greg quotes Jesus' statements on judging and on limitless forgiveness. How often must sinners, including priests, be forgiven? Seven times – or seventy seven times? Even those who stay during the Mass do not approach Fr Greg to receive communion. It is only the young girl who had been abused who comes to him and the film ends with their tearful embrace.

Jimmy McGovern dramatises the crises but offers no solutions except understanding and forgiveness. A similar Catholic perspective (from Ireland) on celibacy, sexual orientation, AIDS and ecclesiastical double standards is found in John Deery's *Conspiracy of Silence* (2003).

The Crime of Father Amaro

Celibacy and double standards were headlined in the Mexican film, *El Crimen del Padre Amaro* (2002), nominated for an Oscar for Best Foreign film. It stars the versatile Gael García Bernal, whose impersonation of a young priest is accurate in its style. The dialogue he is given also reflects the kind of 'in' dialogue in priestly circles. It is not a film to be ignored or simply dismissed as offensive.

The plot of *The Crime of Fr Amaro* is to some extent commonplace for Latin America, where celibacy is not infrequently honoured in the breach rather than the observance. This means that Latin American society is more open and direct about clerical behaviour than, for instance, English-speaking societies (the pressure on the parish priest in *Priest*).

Fr Amaro, newly-ordained, is the very model of the desired young priest. He has worked as secretary for the bishop and shown himself to be devoted, diligent and shrewd. He is destined for further studies in Rome in Moral Theology. He is comfortably clerical in dress and demeanour, but is also comfortable in wearing ordinary clothes as became the custom for so many clergy after Vatican II.

But, he is tested in the parish. Like Fr Greg in *Priest*, he discovers that his parish priest is no shining light. Then he himself is attracted to a pious young catechist (daughter of the parish priest's mistress), who has a heavy crush on him. He begins an affair. He lies. He ultimately pressures her to have an abortion during which she dies. His ecclesiastical prospects and career are more important to him than love and honesty. In the meantime, he delivers the bishop's dismissal to a priest who lives and works with the people and who has fallen foul of local landowners and drug lords (whose money is laundered while supporting the building of a Catholic hospital). It is this priest who lives his vocation but who is condemned – and who opts to stay working with the poor. It was in Latin America that the phrase 'fundamental option for the poor' originated, a phrase that has been taken up as a war-cry by some and as inspiration for many first world organisations.

Fr Amaro could have been a fine priest but he was too young, too immature, too pampered, too pedestalled, too ambitious. Fr Greg admitted his sins and failings and wanted to find solace and a solution within his vocation. Fr Amaro could not admit his sins and compounded them while using his vocation as a safety net against any accusations. Because of the now seemingly unlimited discussion about priesthood, its strengths and its weaknesses, both the Fr Greg story and the Fr Amaro story colour any consideration of the priesthood and its image today.

The Millennium Clergy

While the image of the clergy was open to greater critique than ever in the late 1990s and seminaries were reporting little intake of students for the priesthood, one aspect of priestly life, a rather esoteric aspect akin to *The Exorcist* but more mind-blowing, was emerging on screen as the millennium approached. The priest was now a strange kind of hero, being set up to confront the forces of evil that manifested themselves in striking, computergraphic and special effects ways. Alongside these adventurer priests was a range of highly placed bishops and cardinals, who used their power in the church to preserve their church no matter what it took. By the year 2000, audiences who delighted in this kind of ecclesiastical-horror-action show could have seen, among others, *Stigmata, End of Days, John Carpenter's Vampires, Resurrection, The Body*. A few years later came *The Sin Eater* and *Van Helsing*. (This was also the period when fundamentalist groups in the United States made apocalyptic films like *The Omega Code* and *Left Behind*.)

This is Dan Brown territory. Millions have read his *Angels and Demons* and, particularly, *The Da Vinci Code*. Combining the cosmic conspiracy conventions of popular authors like Robert Ludlum (conspiracies for evil world domination in politics and finance) and Dean Koontz (conspiracies for overwhelming evil supernatural domination), Brown invents cosmic religious conspiracies. He makes them plausible with allegedly authentic scientific detail and allegedly accurate presentation of the Catholic Church, though his grasp of the workings of the Catholic Church remains at a vividly surface level. His novels provide a page-turning read, but would not stand up to rigorous textual examination. Nor do these films. They purport to be the truth (about the Gospel of Thomas and

Jesus' saying that the church was to be an inner personal experience as at the end of *Stigmata*) or give biblical references (which are inexact as at the end of *The Body*). Rather, they are stimulating movies that critics deride and audiences enjoy.

They also gave some of the next generation of actors their chance to be screen priests. Gabriel Byrne was the hero of *Stigmata*, Antonio Banderas of *The Body*, Heath Ledger and Mark Addy in *The Sin Eater*. Rod Steiger was the exception. Having been the priest in *The Amityville Horror*, he now gave Arnold Schwarzennegger the information he needed to combat the devil on the evening of 31 December 1999, at 11.55pm. Alongside of them were unscrupulous bishops and cardinals, Jonathan Pryce in *Stigmata*, Peter Weller in *The Sin Eater* and Cardinal Maximilian Schell losing his faith and trying for immortality as one of the living dead in *John Carpenter's Vampires*.

These movies are not highly significant contributions to looking at the screen image of the priest. However, they are quite widely seen, especially by younger fans. While they are OK for entertainment, they create an image of clergy that bears little relationship to a priest's everyday life (one hopes!).

Primal Fear

Judgment, the HBO movie on the 1980s Louisiana sex abuse case, was screened in 1990. There was an ambiguous Italian movie in 1996, *Pianese Nunzio*. The Neapolitan Mafia want to destroy a local priest critic. He is emotionally involved with the nearly 14-year-old young Nunzio and this is used against him. However, the Italians, at least in the mid-1990s, seem to have had a less condemnatory view of the issue than what was emerging in English-speaking countries.

By 2002, 2003, 2004, scenes of the sexual abuse of minors by priests or members of religious orders were included in three films, *The Magdalene Sisters* (2002), a Scottish film set in the Catholic laundry institutions of Dublin in the mid-1960s and *Song for A Raggy Boy* (2003), an Irish film set in a

Christian Brothers' reformatory school in 1939. The brief abuse sequence in *Raggy Boy* is all the more powerful and horrifying for those who see the film because so much of the discussion about the issue by those who are not immediately involved remains on an abstract level. At this level, it is easy to deny or dismiss allegations of abuse as exaggerated. *Raggy Boy*, with its characters and story, makes the abuse real.

Pedro Almodóvar included this theme in his *Mal Educación* (Bad Education) (2004). Almodóvar's clever and complex film is about a fictional short story and its screen version, based on a memoir, and what actually happened to the characters. The movie does not shirk the reality of a priest abusing a boy and how this was handled by Spanish church authorities. What it does show, in a way that the Irish films do not, is the emotional response of the priest concerned. The boy is invited by the college community of priests to come to the priests' dining room to sing for the rector's birthday dinner. The rapt look of the rector, oblivious to everything else around him and, probably, to his own immature infatuation with the boy, takes audiences back to the perpetrator and puzzlement about his psychology.

A popular Hollywood movie of 1996 that raised abuse issues was *Primal Fear*. It starred Richard Gere and Laura Linney as lawyers who become involved in the trial for the murder of the Archbishop of Chicago. Edward Norton gives a fascinating performance as the young accused. What is revealed is that the Archbishop is a pornography addict. He uses young, unemployed men and women to act out sexual experiences while they are being videotaped. It seems that he has been attacked and stabbed by one of the participants in these filmings.

The bulk of the film consists of the investigation and the court case. However, it was shocking in the mid-1990s to see the behaviour of the archbishop. But it linked in with what was emerging in the United States Church and what was to emerge about sexual misconduct even on the part of some bishops who had to resign their office. *Primal Fear* was made just fifty years after *Going My Way* seemed to show the norms for clerical life and behaviour and won its Oscars. This means that movies had changed in what they felt they could dramatise. It means that the Churches had to examine their consciences, acknowledge sinfulness and guilt, be prepared to face civil trials and penalties and to atone for these sins.

In 2005, American cable channel, Showtime, produced *Our Fathers*. The year 2002 was a most difficult year for the Catholic Church in the United States. Many victims of clerical sexual abuse and molestation made themselves known to authorities, especially after the court proceedings against Fr John Geoghan in Boston. It was a harrowing year for these victims with their memories and hurt and for their families. It was also a harrowing year for many in authority in the Church, from bishops to diocesan directors of communication who had to find ways of responding to media demands while always offering compassion to those who suffered. It was a year of apologies. It was a year of judicial proceedings and attempts to formulate appropriate protocols for the American Church.

Our Fathers, directed by Dan Curtis, and based on the book, *Our Fathers: the Secret Life of the Catholic Church in an Age of Scandal*, by David France, who had covered the story when a senior editor at *Newsweek*, is a dramatised interpretation of the year in Boston which began with the Fr Geoghan trial, continued with other priests being accused and ended with the resignation of Cardinal Bernard Law. The film is generally carefully written, giving voice to a range of perspectives, questions and attitudes that have emerged in connection with the sex abuse cases. The legal aspects of the case are frequently centre screen. As might be expected, the film is supportive of victims and critical of church authorities, personalities and procedures.

Our Fathers shows the victims of abuse in their adult years and the damage that they still bear, ranging from low self-esteem and marital difficulties, even to suicide. Sometimes Catholics who have not personally encountered someone who has experienced abuse are not really aware of the consequences of the abuse and the long-term spiritual and psychological damage – and alienation from priests and the church. They are not aware of the constant feelings of shame and self-blame that the victims retain. *Our Fathers* uses discreetly filmed flashbacks (with the emphasis on verbal communication rather than visuals of the molestations) to bring home the reality of the abuse within the context of family life, school, church and the plausible pretexts that the clergy used to deceive parents and rationalise their behaviour with the children.

In dramatic terms, one of the most moving sequences has an adult character remember his experiences with Fr Birmingham and then reveal to his fellow victims that he had visited the priest as he was dying in hospital thirteen years earlier to find some kind of forgiveness for his hatred of him.

Christopher Plummer appears as Cardinal Law. He interprets the Cardinal in a complex way. He is a churchman of the old school who sees it as his duty to protect the church and its reputation. He is a prelate who comes to realise that he has made grave mistakes in judgment – the scene where he speaks of his mistakes to Pope John Paul II has moving moments and takes us into the mind and heart of the Cardinal. The other sequences that repay viewing to try to understand how the Cardinal saw his role include a visit of one of the victims (who has been ignored and put off even when the Cardinal had said he would meet victims) confronts him in his residence and forces the Cardinal to listen and empathise as well as persuading him to attend a meeting of victims and families where he has a tough reception.

Our Fathers shows how the sins of the fathers affect their victims, who need compassion, and how they affect all those who belong to the church.

Recovering the image of the priest and the vocation to the priesthood

The age-old prayer of the Churches is to ask God for more vocations to priesthood and the religious life. Dioceses and orders appointed Vocation Directors to recruit candidates. Junior schools took in young men who thought they might have a vocation. Novitiates in the 1950s and early 1960s were full. Seminaries were overflowing, with many new seminaries being built. That began to change in the late 1960s. While many people still devoutly pray for vocations, God does not seem to be calling men and women as in previous generations. There are new movements within the church that are attracting more members than the traditional orders and dioceses. Some are devout. Some are involved in ministry. Some are more geared to life within the church. Many of these are more traditional in their theology and their lifestyles. The Catholic Church is a broad church, like the many mansions that Jesus refers to in his father's house. Is it possible for there to be a return to the old days?

There are some positive images of priesthood alongside the questioning and the critique.

PHASE FOUR:
Positive images of priesthood

The Mission

In the mid-1980s there was a moment of reprieve in questioning the screen priest's image. It was *The Mission* (1986). Directed by Roland Joffé, who had just had a great success with *The Killing Fields*, *The Mission* found a wider audience than was anticipated. It also received several Oscar nominations including that of Best Film and for Ennio Morricone's evocative score. The screenplay was written by Robert Bolt, not a Christian, but a writer who had great admiration for the heroic religious conscience, He was the author of the play and film about St Thomas More, *A Man for All Seasons*.

In the context of eighteenth-century mission villages in South America, the so-called Jesuit Reductions, priests were presented as heroic. These men had given up everything to be at the service of the Indians. The film opens with a priest being martyred, crucified by the Indians and the cross pushed over a waterfall. This spectacular scene was used for advertising and on the jacket for the video release. They were committed and dedicated priests.

Two very different priests are at the centre of *The Mission*. Fr Gabriel (Jeremy Irons) is portrayed as a gentle man, seeking out the Indians, a musician who charmed like a devout Pied Piper. Another character, Rodrigo Mendoza (Robert de Niro), is seen first as a slave dealer, ruthlessly patient in capturing the Indians. He undergoes a conversion experience, literally having to let go the worldly possessions burdening his back as he tries to climb a cliff. He is not the easy community man that Fr Gabriel is and clashes with the Jesuit authorities. This is finally put to the test when the Spanish and Portuguese attack the Indians (given leave by the sinister diplomatic ecclesiastic, Altamirano (Ray McAnnally), whose quiet and deadly speeches open and close the film. What are the priests to do?

In many ways, the priests in *The Mission* dramatise the dilemma of many clergy in South America in the 1970s and 1980s. The movement called Liberation Theology, condemned by many authorities as too Marxist to be Catholic, endorsed the Church's option for the poor, for creating 'basic Christian communities' where everyone would pray and live the Gospel message, and for opposing civil repression. Fr Gabriel is the priest who stays with his people to the end. They are massacred in front of the Church, he holding the monstrance containing the body of Christ. This is the response of the martyrs. De Niro, on the other hand, goes out to fight side by side with the Indians and dies of wounds inflicted in defence of justice. This is the response of those who want to be liberators.

Three years later, a movie portrait of the contemporary martyr for justice in Latin America, Archbishop Oscar Romero of El Salvador (assassinated in 1980) was released, *Romero* (1989). Romero was in the background of Oliver Stone's *Salvador* (1986) and *Choices of the Heart* (1983), the story of American lay missionary, Jean Donovan, and the sisters executed by the Salvadoran military in 1980. In that film, Martin Sheen appeared as Jean's priest adviser. In 1991, there was a version of Brian Moore's novel, *Black Robe*, the story of the Jesuit missionaries in Canada in 1634. This is a tougher movie than *The Mission*. The Jesuit priest, Fr Laforgue (Lothaire Bluteau) comes from a French spirituality that is severe, ascetical and cerebral, adjectives that could describe many a very serious priest. Fr Laforgue goes on a journey in the harsh landscapes, experiences torture by the Indians, reaches a distant mission where he has to learn to love the Indians he serves or his mission will be meaningless. It was a strange choice of subject for the early 1990s movie-going public and it was not widely seen – which is a pity because it offers a strong and challenging image of the priest.

Mass Appeal

This was the nicely witty title of a popular American play from the early 1980s, released as a film in 1985. It starred Jack Lemmon as a very convincing priest. While it echoes the questions of the period, it is still very relevant in any consideration of church and priesthood (and suggests issues in seminary training, especially concerning sexual behaviour and orientation that were to become even more important and taxing during the 1990s).

The drama at the centre of *Mass Appeal* is the approval or not of a deacon, Mark Dolan (Zelko Ivanek), to go on to ordination, his ministerial apprenticeship in the parish of Fr Tim Farley (Jack Lemmon) and the challenge he offers to Fr Farley, who has grown complaisant in his priestly work.

Mark Dolan is not the eager young innocent seminarian of thirty years earlier. He grew up in the 70s and its experimentation. However, he wants to serve as a celibate priest. The 70s also encouraged him to be something of a firebrand, especially in the pulpit. Sensitivity is not his number one attribute. That is something Fr Farley encourages in him. He is prepared to clash with the rather bull-headed rector of the seminary Monsignor Thomas Burke (Charles Durning), especially over what he considers matters of natural justice. Fr Dolan is an image of the priest who could respond to the needs of the times, once he learned empathy, and could incorporate that into his down-to-earth ministry.

However, it is Fr Farley who deserves attention. He is a good man. He is at the service of his parishioners. But, he lives in a comfortable parish. He is respected by everyone. He has status among the clergy. He has taken his priesthood for granted and discovers how much he needs to be shaken out of his easy satisfaction with his performance. This is the portrait of the average priest of those and later times. He is relied on, expected to be at the beck and call of everyone, to be a prayerful man, a man who preaches God's word and touches his congregation's minds and hearts. He is a candidate for burnout.

In a scene that anticipates the finale of *Priest*, Fr Farley begins the celebration of Mass. He stops, feels he can't go on. In a confession to his parishioners, he explains the situation with Mark and the seminary rector, but he also confesses himself, his inadequacies, his self-absorption, stating that Mark is already a far better priest than he is. After that confession, he is ready to celebrate the Mass.

Whatever image of priest is seen on screen, positive or negative, the priest who acknowledges the truth about his limitations, yet who perseveres with his work, is one that people are glad to see. This is no priest who relies on status, who tries to avoid hypocrisy.

Keeping the Faith

It is clear that this chapter is moving towards a positive image of priesthood amid the sometimes chaotic responses to the priesthood in our times. It is only four decades since the demand for updating and renewal of priestly ministry was asked for at the Second Vatican Council. This is, of course, a very short time in the overall scheme of things. While change can seem to happen very quickly, overall this is not the case. Human beings move more slowly. They also get older and tired. They lose energy. As the clergy who emerged from the 1960s age and retire, they see that the face of the church in the pews has changed (or, more accurately, there are fewer faces there). Who will be the parish priests of 2010, let alone 2020? Who will be available to become bishops? There is a myriad of questions: what of part-time priests with particular ministry to a limited local group? Will the celibacy requirement be changed – ironically (and hurtfully to many priests) those who are not obliged to celibacy are those married priests who come from other denominational churches? And, the ordination of women...?

The final movie for consideration has a morale-boosting title, *Keeping the Faith* (2000). It is a surprise of a movie, seemingly unthinkable for a Hollywood production at the beginning of the twenty-first century. It is the story of three friends who grow up in New York City. One becomes a rabbi for whom married status is essential (Ben Stiller). One becomes a priest for whom marriage is impossible (Edward Norton, who also directed the movie). The third is the young girl who disappeared to the West Coast when they were eight, but has now returned as a successful executive. Audiences will have little trouble in guessing what happens. Well, yes and no.

Clearly, the screenplay has the young priest falling in love with his childhood friend, but it is not in the vein of the tortured souls in *True Confessions* or *Priest*. He deals with the situation realistically, discusses it with the woman, with his rabbi friend (who is actually in a relationship with the woman) and, especially, with his parish priest. The parish priest is played by veteran Czech director, Milos Forman. He is given a wise scene where he talks about the difficulties of the celibate life, yet not in any self-pitying way. Yes, he has fallen in love – and often. But he has still lived his commitment and has done so for decades. Priesthood and celibacy are possible, not easy but possible. The movie's screenplay takes this for granted. Yet, *Keeping the Faith* is no propaganda for this way of life. It assumes that this is the way the Catholic Church is. It shows priests who struggle but who can live through their struggles and be effective ministers. (The Jewish-Catholic friendship also offers image of practical interfaith collaboration: a club for the older members of both congregations.)

For many priests, *Keeping the Faith* was something of a breather. It paid respect to their lives. It tried to dramatise the day-by-day reality of priesthood and its relevance to the contemporary world. It did not preclude changes in the celibacy requirements in the future.

The priest and the future

First of all, the past forty years have seen extraordinary and unanticipated changes in the way that priests are selected, trained and live their ministry. In the western countries, very few men are choosing priesthood as a way of life (or, to phrase it more religiously, God does not seem to be choosing many men for priesthood). It is different in Africa, Asia and parts of Latin America. The numbers entering seminaries are very high. One question comes up: will the patterns of the West eventually be repeated in these other continents? The traditions of sexuality in many of these countries militate against the observance of celibacy. Men make heroic efforts, but there have been many scandals and, often, bishops have overlooked these scandals, conscious that they do not have enough priests to meet the pastoral demands in the parishes of their dioceses.

Secondly, with the decline in church attendance for whatever reason (loss of a sense of community, loss of a sense of obligation, attitudes of laziness or couldn't care less, liturgy being remote or boring, trivial or boring preaching), so many younger people do not see priests in any regular way. Images of the priest come from past experiences, both good and bad (but it seems to be the bad that are best remembered), from what is handed down as family or parental wisdom, from media headlines that have been devastating, from hearsay and gossip... and from the movies.

This chapter has offered a checklist of the screen images of priests they may have seen, to try to situate them in their times and to evaluate how accurate they are. And now we wait for movies with screen priests played by Brad Pitt, Johnny Depp, Tom Cruise. We need not add Sean Penn because he played a bogus priest with Robert de Niro in *We're No Angels* (1989), criminals in disguise. But then his character really did enter a monastery...

Afterword

This book has attempted to open up several significant and relevant areas where the movies meet the concerns of audiences today. It is a beginning. I hope that the ideas and the movies discussed will lead to greater understanding of the movies themselves but also of the issues they dramatise and how they do this by way of audiovisual storytelling. It means that there are many more contemporary questions to be raised, many more values to be explored.

In my own work, I have had the opportunity to follow several leads which have proven fruitful in this dialogue between movies and morality. In a long time of reviewing films, I have been able to listen to a great deal of feedback and critique which, I hope, I have absorbed. Another source of feedback has been the interviews with film directors, especially Australian directors, hearing their approaches to values – and their spirituality.

A more explicit way of considering the religious implications of movies is via the Christ-figure. There are plenty of Jesus-movies for an explicit look at the Gospel story of Jesus, Jesus-figures. But there are many characters in movies who, consciously or unconsciously, have been created to resemble Jesus significantly and substantially. These are the Christ-figures. We realise that, while Steven Spielberg wanted ET to be like Peter Pan, his screenwriter, Melissa Mathison, drew on her background of the Gospel story of Jesus coming to earth; 'then I noticed the Jesus resemblances', she said.

In recent decades, many directors have been including religious iconic material in their films. For Christian reference, this is especially in the use of the crucifix as a symbol of suffering and redemption. Martin Scorsese with his Catholic background does it. Steven Spielberg, with his Jewish background, has done it, significantly in *Amistad*.

Lately, I have been involved in what I have called 'A Movie Lectionary'. It was suggested that I find a popular movie which related to the Sunday Gospel readings in the common Christian lectionary. American publishing know-how decided to call the series, *Lights Camera? Faith!* With over 200 movies considered for the three volumes, I am convinced that there is a fruitful dialogue between the movies and the biblical texts and themes. In the United States, similar books and guides have proliferated meaning that this approach makes a great deal of religious sense and talks the language that people are comfortable with. It has also meant that we have been exploring Lights Camera Faith for The Ten Commandments and, more recently, The Beatitudes and the Seven Deadly Sins.

Yes, I do believe, strongly, that movies can be moral and spiritual compasses.

Peter Malone

The World Association for Christian Communication

The World Association for Christian Communication (WACC) promotes communication for social change. It believes that communication is a basic human right that defines people's common humanity, strengthens cultures, enables participation, creates community, and challenges tyranny and oppression. WACC's key concerns are media diversity, equal and affordable access to communication and knowledge, media and gender justice, and the relationship between communication and power. It tackles these through advocacy, education, training, and the creation and sharing of knowledge. WACC's worldwide membership works with faith-based and secular partners at grassroots, regional and global levels, giving preference to the needs of the poor, marginalised and dispossessed. Being WACC means 'taking sides'.

World Association for Christian Communication (WACC)
357 Kennington Lane
London SE11 5QN
United Kingdom
Tel: +44 (0)20 7582 9139
www.wacc.org.uk